ESTEVANICO THE BLACK

WESTERNLORE GREAT WEST AND INDIAN SERIES
XXXVI

BOOKS BY JOHN UPTON TERRELL

TRADERS OF THE WESTERN MORNING — Aboriginal Commerce in Pre-Columbian North America

FAINT THE TRUMPET SOUNDS — The Life and Trials of Major Reno

WAR FOR THE COLORADO RIVER — 2 Volumes

JOURNEY INTO DARKNESS — The Story of Cabeza de Vaca

BLACK ROBE — A Biography of the Noted Explorer-Missionary, Father DeSmet

FURS BY ASTOR — The History of John Jacob Astor and the American Fur Trade

PLUME ROGUE — A Novel of the Western Pathfinders

PUEBLO OF THE HEARTS — Story of Pueblo de los Corazones

SUNDAY IS THE DAY YOU REST — Novel of the Southwest

THE LITTLE DARK MAN — A Novel of the Cattle Trails

For Younger Readers

THE KEY TO WASHINGTON

THE DEPARTMENT OF THE INTERIOR

THE DEPARTMENT OF THE TREASURY

THE DEPARTMENT OF STATE

THE DEPARTMENT OF HEALTH, EDUCATION, AND WELFARE

THE DEPARTMENT OF JUSTICE

THE DEPARTMENT OF AGRICULTURE

THE DEPARTMENT OF COMMERCE

THE DEPARTMENT OF DEFENSE

THE DEPARTMENT OF THE POST OFFICE

THE DEPARTMENT OF LABOR

Ruins of Hawikuh

— *John Upton Terrell Photos.*

JOHN UPTON TERRELL

ESTEVANICO THE BLACK

WESTERNLORE PRESS, PUBLISHERS
1968 . . . Los Angeles 90041

To Donna —

In Memory of a Windy Day
at Hawikuh . . .

AUTHOR'S NOTE

WHILE I was writing this book, I was taken to task in a discussion about Southwestern history by a woman member of an organization purportedly dedicated to commemorating historical events.

She was disturbed by my remark that Fray Marcos of Nice was not the first foreign explorer to enter Arizona and New Mexico, and was not the discoverer of the so-called Kingdom of the Seven Cities of Cibola, as so many general histories lead one to believe.

The first man of Old World blood to traverse the region, I added, was Estevanico the Black. He went ahead of Fray Marcos from Mexico, crossed Arizona, and reached Hawikuh, the most westerly pueblo of Cibola, in New Mexico, and several days' journey beyond the padre's farthest point of advance.

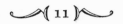

"I think you are very much mistaken in giving him the credit," she said in indignation. "Estevanico was nothing but a Negro slave obeying orders."

Two things are wrong with her contention. Estevanico most certainly was not obeying orders, and the word *nothing* is most inappropriate.

In defiance of all instructions given him by Fray Marcos, he plunged ahead to open the land gate to the American Southwest. And he paid with his life for his disobedience and his daring. That seems to me to be *something*.

I know of no memorial to Estevanico the Black. No national monument, no river, no highway, no mountain peak, is named for him. Most school histories say very little about him, if, indeed, they mention him at all.

He was a Moor. Therefore, he was not a Christian. Yet, he did not hesitate to make the sign of the cross or to mutter Hail Marys or to count beads. At the same time, he carried a sacred Indian gourd rattle and he danced to Indian gods. Therefore, he was a blasphemer and a hypocrite, as well as a disbeliever and an infidel.

He took Indian women to his robes, and he got drunk and howled and laughed away hours about campfires with painted warriors, and he told wild untrue tales. Therefore, he was immoral, a voluptuary, an inebriate and a liar.

But one who cares to look far enough will find assets that go toward bringing the books more into balance.

He spoke several Indian tongues. He talked fluently with his hands in the language of the signs. He was a wilderness diplomat *par excellence*, until that fateful day at Hawikuh. He had the manner of a big black friendly dog. He was loyal throughout his life to his owners. He was incomparably courageous. He was trusted and respected by hundreds of Indians in numerous tribes between the Gulf of Mexico and the Gulf of California, between the mountains of Sonora and the Valley of Mexico, and he was revered by many of them.

And he was much more.

With Cabeza de Vaca, Andres Dorantes and Alonzo del Castillo, he made the greatest journey into the unknown, into the unmapped wilderness darkness, in North American history ... the first crossing of the Continent from the Atlantic to the Pacific north of Mexico. He was one of the most intrepid, brave, indomitable and accomplished explorers of the New World.

JOHN UPTON TERRELL.

ESTEVANICO THE BLACK

I

HE ENTERED upon the stage of the American mainland in Holy Week, in the year 1528. Contemporary accounts do not name the day he went ashore. Indeed, they do not name him at this time, for of all the men of the Narvaez Expedition few, if any, were lower in station. Yet, there can be no doubt that he was there, that he traveled with his owners from Spain to Santo Domingo, on to Cuba, thence to the land still thought to be an island, called Florida.

Spanish documents and translations of them speak of him as Estevan, Estevanico, Stephen, and on many occasions simply as the Negro or the Black. Cabeza de de Vaca, who first told of him in print, preferred to call him Estevanico the Black, and this seems reason enough to use that name.

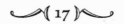

If the day he set foot on the Florida peninsula remains uncertain . . . it was probably Good Friday . . . the place of landing can be reasonably well identified. It was an arm of sand, palmettos and marsh grass just west of Tampa Bay, in the vicinity of Clement's Point and John's Pass.

Inside the arm, the clear placid waters of lagoons spread away like avenues of mirrors into tall dark forests. There the expedition's five vessels . . . four small caravels and a brigantine . . . anchored in safe haven. Outside, the Gulf of Mexico reached westward and was lost in a blending of water and sky, an infinity of hazy blue distance.

Before this April of 1528, no more than a few pale candles had been lighted in the geographical darkness northward from Cuba. A few ships had skirted the Atlantic coast and had poked their prows into some river mouths and bays. In 1513, Juan Ponce de Leon, sailing from Puerto Rico, where he had won a great reputation by slaughtering helpless natives, had reached a "land of flowers." He had found neither the gold nor the youth-giving waters for which he was looking, and being constantly menaced by Indians he had abandoned the search and departed.

In 1519, the noted pilot, Alonso Alvarez de Pineda, had ascertained that the sea west of Ponce de Leon's island of Florida was in fact an immense gulf, and no passage to the Pacific opened from it. In sailing along the Gulf of Mexico shore as far as Vera Cruz he had crossed the mouth of an inconceivably large river flowing from the north. It would be known as the Mississippi.

Ponce de Leon, meanwhile, had become fearful that

usurpers would steal from him the Florida he considered his by right of discovery. Obtaining a royal patent to colonize it, he set out again in 1521. This time he went to the west coast, making a landing near Charlotte Harbor. Again Indians drove his company off. Severely wounded, he fled to Cuba, where he died.

Pinpoints of light flickered on the coasts, but the interior of Florida north of the Gulf shore remained in total darkness, unseen by any European. It was into this unknown that the expedition of Panfilo de Narvaez was going.*

Estevanico was a native of Asemmur, or Azamor, on the west coast of Morocco. Virtually nothing more can be said of his background. The date of his birth has not been definitely determined, but in 1528 he undoubtedly was a young man, probably in his middle or late twenties. There are some good reasons for this assumption: his extraordinary vitality, his unquenchable spirit, his love of revelry, his ability to endure not only the hardships and brutal treatment suffered by slaves, and especially blackamoors, in the Spain of the period, but the terrible ordeals of eight years in an unopened wilderness, years as a captive of low-caste savages, years on a trek that is without equal in the history of American exploration.

Only three other men of the three hundred and one of the Narvaez land expedition survived with him. They were Alvar Nunez Cabeza de Vaca, Andres Dorantes de Carranca, and Alonzo del Castillo Maldonado.

*A detailed account of the Narvaez Expedition is contained in the author's *Journey Into Darkness*. Only incidents connected with it which reflected upon the development of Estevanico's character and influenced the course of his adventures are included in this work.

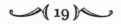

Cabeza de Vaca of Jerez de la Frontera had been appointed an aide to the Duke of Medina Sidonia after three years of military service, during which he had fought against the French at Bologna and Ferrara, and had been badly wounded at Ravenna. His record as an officer of exceptional ability and unquestionable integrity had won him the post of Treasurer of the Narvaez Expedition. In this capacity he was responsible for collecting the king's five per cent of all precious metals and stones obtained. He also was obligated to report as to how obediently and efficiently all royal decrees were carried out. Perhaps to be more certain that he had adequate authority to perform these important duties, the Spanish Court ordered that he also serve as Provost-Marshal, an office which placed him in charge of military discipline.

Castillo of Salamanca was the son of a doctor. He had been well educated and had been reared as a gentleman, but he had not always in his life acted like one. He was addicted to gambling, and he had been involved in several unpleasant situations with women of doubtful character. However, he was both courageous and daring, and he had won his captaincy in the cavalry on the field of battle.

When Estevanico was taken to Spain from his homeland, and how he became the property of Dorantes, are mysteries which may never be solved. Dorantes was a member of a family which enjoyed some degree of prominence in Estremadura. He had received a commission as a captain of infantry on the recommendation of Don Alvaro de Zuniga, Duke of Bejar. Upon joining the company of Narvaez he was assigned a post and responsibilities commensurate with his rank. That he elected to take Estevanico with him on the long and hazardous journey indicates his appreciation of the slave's trustworthiness and ability.

Panfilo de Narvaez was tall, courtly, proud, well-mannered, arrogant, inept, stubborn, stupid, and possessed of inordinate greed. He had a voice that was deep and resonant, and under pressure of anger sounded as if it were coming out of a cave. He had lost an eye in a fight with the men of Cortez in Mexico, and he wore a silk patch over the empty socket. After that misfortune, his surviving orb had developed a fierce and penetrating gleam.

He was an old hand in the Indies when he landed his expedition near Tampa Bay, having spent more than twenty years there in His Majesty's service. Mines, lands, concessions and privileges awarded him for his successful campaigns had made him wealthy. Deservedly he was acclaimed as one of the most proficient butchers of natives among the many *conquistadores* who possessed outstanding talent in this field of enterprise.

The governorship of Florida had remained vacant since the death of Ponce de Leon until Narvaez secured it. The northern boundary of the territory over which the office gave him jurisdiction could not be delineated, simply because no one knew where it might be. The southern extent of the province was easier to define. It was the Gulf of Mexico shore, all the way from the Florida Keys to the River de las Palmas, north of the present city of Tampico. Somewhere within this vast reach Narvaez was, by royal command, to establish two permanent settlements, and to build three forts.

Narvaez established nothing, except a trail of terrible tragedies. He accomplished nothing, except a disaster. The only achievements with which he may be credited were extraordinary displays of unmitigated cowardice and incompetence. On several occasions his life was saved by the self-sacrifice of his men, but when some of them, weakened and near death, needed the assistance of his hardier personal staff members he demonstrated his contemptible selfishness by rejecting their plea for help.

II

IT WAS on May 1, 1528, over the strenuous protests of
Cabeza de Vaca and other officers, that Narvaez abandoned his ships, and with two hundred and sixty men
on foot and forty of horses marched into the interior,
northward from Old Tampa Bay.

This was the first overland expedition on American
soil.

Only four of the three hundred men would ever again
enter a civilized community: Cabeza de Vaca, Castillo,
Dorantes, and Estevanico the Black.

Crazed by a craving for fortune that would surpass
that gained by Cortez in Mexico, which he had seen
with his one sharp eye, Narvaez began the journey into
the unknown wilderness without plan or adequate
preparation. Not only did he not know what types of

country lay ahead or what native forces he would be obliged to face, but his stores permitted the distribution to each man of only two pounds of biscuit and half a pound of bacon.

There is only one authoritative account of the incomparable journey. It is the *Relacion* which Cabeza de Vaca wrote after reaching Mexico in 1536. Other documents pertaining to the expedition contain the same material in part, or stem from this famous narrative. In it the name of Estevanico the Black was first brought to the attention of the world.

As Narvaez and his company moved into the Florida wastelands, plumes and banners waved in the damp tropical breeze. Breastplates and arms gleamed in the sunlight. Strung out in a long line, weaving through the scrub growth, palmettos and reeds, the soldiers with their weapons, knives girding thighs, and the horsemen with lances aloft and swords rattling an accompaniment to the jingling of spur chains, presented a formidable array.

The officers and gentlemen were grand in their colorful costumes. Fluttering bright silks, shining soft leather boots, glittering armor, fine linens, silver buttons and gay plumes adorned them, and in their personal luggage were thick woolen blankets, down coverlets, and capes of heavy cloth and soft fur.

Somewhere along the line was a little band of padres, a dream of many conversions to come lighting their eyes, a prayer for the success and salvation of the company on their lips. Their cassocks gathered dust and burrs as they plodded dutifully and hopefully along.

On the column moved, toward the northeast, skirting

the northern end of Old Tampa Bay. On through the sandy reaches, splashing through the swamplands, the saw grass cutting the fine boots and the sandals of the padres and the bare feet of the servants, tearing their clothes, slashing their hands and faces, and the mud tarnishing the bright armor. On through the endless stretches of palmettos, the jungle thickets, the pine forests and palm groves, wading, plunging, struggling through the dark waters of uncountable lagoons and streams.

Silence pressed upon them, a silence broken only by bird calls, by their own voices, by the snorts of the Andalusian horses, by the rattle of sabers. It was the silence of the ages, the silence never before interrupted by a foreign invader, the silence of the unknown. It drew a curtain about them, and it swallowed them.

The Indians watched, but for more than a fortnight they offered no resistance. It was as if they fully understood what ordeals the Spaniards would suffer in the verminous, miserable country; privations and hardships no less harrowing and deadly than those of battle.

The first skirmish with natives came in mid-May at the Withlacoochee River. Timuquan Indians attacked and quickly retreated, but several were captured, and probably in the hope of saving themselves they offered to serve as guides. Presumably these captives were the first persons to tell Narvaez of a province called Apalachen, far to the north, which they said contained a city marvelously rich in gold and jewels.

No mention of Estevanico is made thus far in Cabeza de Vaca's *Relacion,* but there is no doubt that he was there.

On the weary column pressed toward Apalachen, enduring terrible hunger, existing largely on the maize and fish confiscated in villages from which the inhabitants had fled. The Spaniards were not woodsmen. Most of them had never seen a jungle before reaching the Indies. They were poor hunters. In a country abounding with wild game, they were unable to provide themselves with sufficient meat.

Yet, unquenchable self-esteem, irrepressible confidence and indestructible visions of glories to come provided the strength to carry them on ... until they saw Apalachen.

It consisted of forty thatched huts. It was dirty, dilapidated and deserted.*

The great dream was shattered with heart-sickening reality. The Apalachees, seeming to sense the despondency of the invaders, launched a series of attacks which took a serious toll.

This was the first sustained warfare between Indians and whitemen on territory that would become a part of the United States.

The Apalachees were renowned among surrounding tribes for their fierceness and skill as warriors. They were, wrote Cabeza de Vaca, so "effectual in their maneuvering that they can receive very little injury." They soon learned how to keep out of range of the crossbows and harquebuses and the clumsy matchlocks, armament which, as Cabeza de Vaca significantly pointed out, was of little value in fighting an enemy which refused to stay longer than a moment in one place, which slipped

*The village was on the shore of Lake Miccosukee, a few miles from Tallahassee.

through the thickets with the quietness of rabbits and the speed of deer.

It was not the guns, not the Spanish bows, not the Spaniards themselves, the Indians feared most. It was the horse. They dreaded the horse, and they fled in consternation from it.

After Apalachen was reached, the disintegration and destruction of the Narvaez Expedition advanced with increasing speed. The retreat became a rout. The Indians maintained an almost incessant assault, striking suddenly from the front, on the flanks, from the rear, and always vanishing into the forests and tall grass as swiftly and as silently as they had come.

In this manner the Spaniards fought their way toward the south. Late in July they reached the deserted village of Aute. It stood near the head of St. Marks Bay. The supply of maize, squash, roots and fish found there would not long sustain them. Seventeen men and a dozen horses had been killed, and more than a score of officers and soldiers were suffering from wounds.

"It was piteous and painful to witness our perplexity and distress," says the *Relacion*. "There was not anywhere to go."

III

AUTE's location offered very little protection, but the Spaniards rested there two days. Then Narvaez requested Cabeza de Vaca "to go and look for the sea."

Still the *Relacion* does not mention Estevanico, but here it does speak of Dorantes as going on the mission to examine the country and find the coast of the open sea.

With Cabeza de Vaca on the assignment were seven men on horseback and fifty on foot. As Dorantes was one of them, it may be assumed that Estevanico accompanied his master. "We traveled until the hour of vespers," Cabeza de Vaca wrote, "when we arrived at a road or entrance to the sea. Oysters were abundant, over which the men rejoiced, and we gave thanks to God that he had brought us there. The following morning [August 1, 1528] I sent twenty men to explore the coast and ascertain its direction. They returned the night after, reporting that those creeks and bays were large, and lay so far inland as made it difficult to examine them agreeably to our desires, and that the sea shore was very distant.

"These tidings obtained, seeing our slender means, I went back to the Governor . . . I gave a report of what I had done, and of the embarrassing nature of the country."

The Indians were continuing their assaults. Many of the Spaniards had become victims of fever and dysentery, and lay writhing in agony on the ground. Despite Cabeza de Vaca's discouraging report, Narvaez ordered the evacuation of Aute in the direction of the sea. The march was begun the following morning.

There were not enough horses to carry the sick and wounded. Men staggered along, blinded and babbling incomprehensibly under the scourge of the fever. Others retched and soiled themselves, unable to control their bodily functions. Flies and mosquitos, swarming about them in great clouds, maddened all. The terrible heat of August beat unmercifully upon them.

It was evening when the tortured column, following the route Cabeza de Vaca had taken, reached the oyster-strewn estuary to the sea on which he had camped.

Narvaez, his one eagle eye glazed with sickness, his arrogance gone, ordered all who were able to gather about his bed. Piteously he asked for advice.

Out of the conference emerged a plan. The estuary opened into the sea. It was their only hope of escape. Boats must somehow be constructed.

Incredibly, the boats were built. The little shipyard that was established on an arm of St. Marks Bay was not only the first in the continental United States, but one of the strangest ever known in all the world.

There were workers, but no craftsmen. Only one man had received some training as a carpenter. There were no tools, no iron plates or bars, no forge, no tow, no rigging, and no one knew how to make such things.

There was not sufficient food. Each day sick men died. The Indians were a constant menace, and snipers fired into the camp day and night.

Yet, until the third week in September the boat building continued.

On the 22nd of September, 1528, an incomparable event, one both ludicrous and pitiful, occurred. Five of the most peculiar vessels ever built pushed out of the shallow waters toward the Gulf of Mexico. Crowded into them, crushed together in a helpless condition, were two hundred and forty-two men, many of them dangerously hurt or ill.

Each craft was about thirty-three feet in length, a weird conglomeration of rough pine planks, crudely hewn stays and ribs, horse hides and palm leaves. The masts were debarked trees, the fittings of silver, gold and brass, the rigging of horse hair, the sails odd pieces of clothing and blankets, the anchors stones. Overloaded beyond the most remote degree of safety, the gunwales were hardly more than a foot above water.

In the first boat were Governor Narvaez and forty-eight men. The second boat was in charge of Alonso Enrriquez and carried forty-eight men. In the third boat, commanded by Castillo and Dorantes, rode Estevanico and forty-five other men. Captains Tellez and Penalosa commanded the fourth boat, with forty-five men. Cabeza de Vaca was the captain of the fifth boat, under him forty-eight men.

Now the most disastrous mistake of the whole expedition was made. It was believed that they were closer to Panuco, a small Spanish slaving station on the central coast of Mexico, than to Bahia de la Cruz, Tampa Bay. The truth was that by sailing down the west coast of Florida on a fairly straight course they would have reached their starting point . . . where the ships still waited for them . . . after a voyage of approximately one hundred and eighty miles. Panuco was six times as distant. They started for it, turning westward.

Miraculously, for forty-six days the flimsy, battered, makeshift, leaking boats held together. The coasts of Western Florida, Alabama, Mississippi and Louisiana were passed. Numerous skirmishes with Indians took place, and several men were killed and a large number were wounded.

They met the great fresh water floods of the Mississippi plunging from the channels of its wide delta.*

Early in November the five boats were lost in storms on the Texas coast.

The two craft, carrying Cabeza de Vaca, Castillo, Dorantes and Estevanico, were driven ashore and destroyed on the Velasco Peninsula, adjacent to Galveston Island. The Tellez-Penalosa boat was wrecked between the mouths of the Brazos and Colorado Rivers. Enrriquez's boat foundered off the entrance to Lavaca Bay. Narvaez's boat was swept to sea at night and vanished.

*This was fourteen years before De Soto reached the river. He did not discover it, as histories erroneously state, but was the first to cross it north of its mouth. It had been marked on Spanish charts, although often incorrectly, long before the De Soto Expedition left Spain.

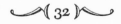

IV

CABEZA DE VACA gave the name Malhado to the island on which his boat and that of Castillo, Dorantes and Estevanico were wrecked . . . the Island of Death. The disasters occurred within a short distance of each other, and the men of the two boats were soon united in a village of the Capoques tribe.

They resigned themselves to spending the winter with the Indians, but, as Cabeza de Vaca recorded, it was "agreed that four men of the most robust should go on to Panuco, which we believed to be near." The four men selected to make the trip took with them an Indian slave who had been brought from Cuba*

*The mission failed, and all five of the men eventually met death in the coastal swamps.

On Malhado Island December came with cruel, cold damp. Storms blew in from a raging gray Gulf. In the flimsy mat houses, the starving Spaniards began to die. At the beginning of the year 1529 only fifteen white men and Estevanico remained alive.*

Now, for the first time in the *Relacion* Cabeza de Vaca speaks of Estevanico by name. With the coming of April, 1529, it was decided that another attempt should be made to reach Panuco by land. Cabeza de Vaca had been stricken with a mysterious malady, and lay near death. Two other men were so feeble that they were unable to travel. The remaining thirteen set out in a desperate attempt to reach safety.

None would succeed, and of the thirteen only Castillo, Dorantes and Estevanico would live to see Cabeza de Vaca again.

The meeting would not take place until the fifth spring after the shipwrecks on Malhado Island.

Cabeza de Vaca recovered slowly from his illness. For a time he had enjoyed a reputation as a healer, but when he had been unable to cure himself the Indians lost faith in his powers, and relegated him to the level of a menial.

For a year he toiled with little relief in this painful subjugation, dutifully responding to the beck and call of his masters. He dug roots from the water until his fingers were so worn that the touch of a straw would cause them to bleed. Broken canes tore his flesh. He gathered wood and built fires and fished and performed

*At this time, the men on the island had no knowledge, of course, of the fate of their comrades who had been in the other three boats. Eventually, the four who were destined to survive would learn that all other members of the expedition had perished.

other chores about the camps, living like a dog to which the Capoques would toss an occasional bone.

It was an almost insupportable life, but he carried on, giving no indication that he was watching always for a means of escape. At last he conceived an ingenious plan which brought him considerable freedom. He had become an expert in the sign language used by the coastal tribes, and he set himself up as a kind of commission merchant and itinerant peddler.

His captors, concluding that he would be more useful to them in such a capacity than as a slave, let him go. With a pack on his back he traveled up and down the coast, as time passed gradually going farther into the interior. Indians gave him orders for articles they desired but which they were unable to obtain for themselves, chiefly because incessant hostilities made it unsafe for them to traverse the country.

He trafficked in cones and sea snails, conch shells which could be used for cutting, other shells used for vessels and decorations, skins, ochre, arrow shafts, sinews, flint and tassels of deer hair. The most valuable of his wares was a small fruit with the appearance of a bean which was used as a stimulant.

He was virtually a free man, and he was highly respected by numerous tribes which were his customers. Why didn't he escape? The opportunity was constantly at hand.

Nothing provides a better understanding of Cabeza de Vaca's character than the reason he continued for four years to peddle his homely commodities. One other man remained alive on Malhado Island. He was Lupe de Oviedo. Cabeza de Vaca remained because he would not desert him.

Each spring he made a special trip to the island to plead with Oviedo to escape with him, but Oviedo was filled with fear, and would not go. Each spring Oviedo promised that he would go with the arrival of the next spring, but it was not until his fifth spring on the island that he found the courage to make the attempt.

In the spring of 1533, the last of the living left the Island of Death.

V

ANDRES DORANTES had been chosen to command the men who set out for Panuco in April, 1529. The little company of thirteen had followed a course close to the coast. Reaching the Brazos River, they had constructed small rafts. The stream was in flood. One of the rafts was swept out to sea, and four men clinging to it had been drowned. At San Antonio Bay another member of the group died, unable to endure longer the diet of crabs and boiled kelp. As they attempted to go on, the remaining eight men were made captives. In the course of several months, five of them met death in various ways, at least two of them by torture and mutilation.

By the fall of 1530, only Castillo, Dorantes and Estevanico remained alive, enduring the cruel treatment and ceaseless labor of slaves.

Dorantes was the first to escape. He made his way some distance inland and reached a village of the

Yguazes tribe. Their brutality surpassed even that which he had suffered before, but he once more managed to flee into the wild. His next haven was with some Mariames, who, although making him a slave, treated him with more consideration.

This was the first time Estevanico had been separated from his owner. He and Castillo remained prisoners of the Indians from whom Dorantes had escaped for a year and a half before they, too, found an opportunity to slip away. Eventually they reached the Mariames and were united with Dorantes.

In was in the spring of 1533 that an Indian informed the three captives that another white man was with a band of Quevenes not far from them. Shortly afterward Cabeza de Vaca suddenly appeared.*

In this way the *Relacion* tells of the reunion:

"When I arrived near their adobe, Andres Dorantes came out to see who it could be ... His astonishment was great when he saw me, as they had for many a day considered me dead ... We gave many things ... and this was a day to us of the greatest pleasure we had enjoyed in life ... Andres Dorantes said that a long time he had entreated Castillo and Estevanico to go forward; but they dared not venture, because they knew not how to swim, and greatly dreaded the rivers and bays they should have to cross, there being many in that country."†

*Shortly after leaving Mulhado Island with Cabeza de Vaca, Lupe de Oviedo, succumbing again to his fears, and perhaps insane, turned back. He was never heard of again. Cabeza de Vaca had gone on alone.

†In view of their past experiences, it was a poor excuse. These were brave men, who placed loyalty and honor, even in the face of death, above other considerations. It seems probable that Castillo and Estevanico were no more willing to desert Dorantes than Cabeza de Vaca had been to leave Oviedo.

Cabeza de Vaca still entertained the idea of escaping in the direction of Panuco. Quickly the others cautioned him against moving hastily or letting the Mariames know of his intentions. They well understood these Indians, and they were in accord in the opinion that any attempt to escape to the south would meet with failure. It was their belief that if they were to have a chance to break for freedom, they must wait at least another six months. At that time the Mariames would move north and west to an area in which prickly pears were abundant. A number of other tribes would travel to the pear fields in the same season. It might then be possible for them to leave with other Indians, perhaps with a tribe that lived to the west, where the Mariames would not venture in an attempt to recapture them.

Although bitterly disappointed at the prospect of another long delay, Cabeza de Vaca accepted their counsel. He and Dorantes became the slaves of the same family, all the members of which were either totally blind or had lost the sight of one eye. Castillo and Estevanico were traded by the Mariames to the Yguazes. Once more the four men were separated.

In the fall of 1533, Indians of various coastal tribes moved inland for the annual pear harvest. Customarily the Mariames and the Yguazes trekked some seventy or eighty miles from their homes near San Antonio Bay.*

Together again, the four men agreed on a plan of escape, selecting a meeting place and setting a night for the break. Once more they were thwarted.

*This would place them in the general vicinity of western Goliad County, or perhaps in Karnes County. Most likely they traveled, at least for part of the journey, up the San Antonio River.

Some Mariames and Yguazes got into a fight over a woman. Fists flew and heads were cracked. When the melee ended, both tribes departed from the scene in brooding anger, taking their slaves with them.

The four men had no alternative but to resign themselves to waiting another year, until the Indians once again returned to the pear fields.

It was another year of drudgery, of mistreatment and often of gnawing hunger.

In the fall of 1534 they were taken once more by their masters to gather pears. Again they made their plans to escape. A rendezvous was set for the night of the full September moon in a prickly pear grove near the San Antonio River.

One by one they slipped away from the Indian camps.

On September 23, 1534, the most daring, difficult and remarkable journey in the history of the New World began.

In simple words the *Relacion* records the event:

"... we commended ourselves to God and set forth with speed, trusting, for all the lateness of the season ... we might still be enabled to travel over a large territory. Hurrying on that day in great dread lest the Indians should overtake us, we saw some smokes, and going on in the direction of them ... we found an Indian. He ran as he discovered us coming ... we sent the negro after him, when he stopped, seeing him alone. The negro told him we were seeking the people who made those fires. He answered that their houses were nearby, and he would guide us to them. So we followed him. He ran to make known our approach, and at sunset we saw the houses ... They were evidently pleased with our com-

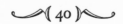

pany ... Dorantes and the negro were lodged in the house of a physician [medicine man], Castillo and myself in that of another."

These Indians Cabeza de Vaca called both Avavares and Chavavares.* Their hospitality convinced the four men that they had reached a safe haven. Cabeza de Vaca wrote that the Avavares had "heard of us before, of our cures, and of the wonders our Lord worked by us."

This statement appears to be a reference to the successful performances of the white men as healers while captives on Malhado Island, for, as far as can be determined from the *Relacion*, they had not acted in the roles of shamans since that time. Whenever it was that the Avavares had received this information, or however it had reached them, they had not forgotten it, and they immediately sought to benefit from the alleged supernatural powers of their guests.

It was during the winter which the four men spent among the Avavares that they achieved true fame as medicine men, and it was at this time that Estevanico's station among them became that of an equal.

If legally he remained a chattel of Dorantes, in reality he was a partner, a colleague, and he was so treated. There were more practical than compassionate reasons for his elevation. The *Relacion* gives the impression that he was big and powerful, that he had the cunning of a panther and the heart of a lion. His untutored mind was shrewd, quick and dangerous. He had a greater facility for learning tongues than the others, and he was a master

*Their linguistic family has not been identified, but it is possible they were Caddoan. They traded with the Mariames, but spoke a different language, although they could understand the Mariames tongue. They seem to have been kindly disposed and were different in habits from the lower coastal tribes.

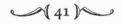

of the sign language. He had already shown a diplomatic ability that gave him great value as an emissary.

If his inherent wildness was hardly less than that of the warriors, he was in no sense a fool. He was willing to learn, to listen to advice and opinions, and in the face of perilous situations he displayed a calmness and wisdom that made him not only reliable but a force to be heeded and admired. He marched on through the wilderness, defying the elements, cursing the dangers and hardships, a pillar of strength, and a monument to the brave of the world.

Cabeza de Vaca was the smallest of the four men. Dignified and gentlemanly, he represented the finest type of officer. Paying tribute to his courage would be anticlimactic. It was unlimited and unqualified. He was kindly and considerate, but these characteristics in no way cast a shadow on his qualifications as a leader. He was highly intelligent, determined and resolute. Never did he abandon his code of honesty and justice, never did he forsake his God, and never did he lose heart under the weight of ordeals that would have crushed most men.

Because the others recognized Cabeza de Vaca's superior intellect, because they knew they could trust him in any situation and under any conditions, because they respected him for his unwavering adherence to his ideals, and because they understood that he held no fear of the vast darkness which lay before them, they made him their captain, and they dutifully obeyed him.

Castillo was the first to be asked by the Avavares to minister to the sick. He was a timid practitioner, not because of a lack of faith but because his own life had not always been commendable, and reviewing it he saw his earthly path marked by irremovable shadows. This oppressive introspection gave rise to the fear in him that he might not continue to enjoy the Lord's favor with the fullness he desired, and which, indeed, he needed. He concluded that it would be unwise to stretch his luck until he had received some sign indicating that the Lord was not yet prepared to punish him for his transgressions. For this reason he attempted to avoid patients who appeared to be seriously afflicted with internal or mental disorders.

When several Indian men complained to him of headaches, he decided it was an ailment he might safely undertake to cure. Over each man he made the sign of the cross and commended him to God. The results of this ministration were instantaneous and amazing. Proclaiming themselves completely cured, the men paid him with pieces of venison, and departed with cries of praise.

Cabeza de Vaca, Dorantes and Estevanico willingly assisted Castillo in wolfing the venison, a delicacy they had seldom enjoyed during their years of captivity. Swiftly word of the miracle spread to adjacent camps. More patients appeared at the door of the clinic. They suffered all manner of illnesses, boils and cramps, diarrhea and ague, blisters and hemorrhoids, indigestion and mental depression, constipation and wens. The halt, the lame, the demented, the healthy and the sane crowded together about the lodge, all pleading for attention, and all proffering pieces of venison.

In the beginning, Dorantes and Estevanico acted mainly in the roles of assistants, or moral supporters, of the besieged Doctors Castillo and Cabeza de Vaca. Dorantes was reticent to practice on his own because he feared he would fail and do injury to both himself and his companions. Estevanico was restrained by the others, for as he was not a Christian they reasoned the Lord would look with disapproval on the idea of a heathen performing rites of a church into which he could not be received.

So many Indians sought relief, however, that the three Catholics were obliged to revise their thinking. In the end they concluded that the Lord would be tolerant enough to forgive Castillo his sins (at least temporarily), kind enough to instill more confidence in Dorantes, and liberal enough to overlook Estevanico's paganism so that the Moor could carry a full share of the case load.

All four became full-fledged shamans, and great was their relief when no chastisements were inflicted upon them from heaven. All four were highly successful.

They had not wanted to spend the winter with the Avavares, but the Avavares convinced them of the folly of attempting to travel either north or west during the cold months. In either of those directions the country was largely uninhabited, except at prickly pear time by traveling tribes, and game was scarce. By this time, of course, they had abandoned the idea of trying to reach Panuco. Their experiences had convinced them that the people who inhabited the miserable land and endured the abominable climate of eastern and southern Texas could be depended upon to do only one thing . . . change. Degenerate, verminous, dwelling in utter degradation, the coastal Indians lived more by instinct than by thought, uncomprehending as animals in their responses to the urges, which dominated them, to feed and fornicate.

In his travels as a peddler, Cabeza de Vaca had come to know that the people of the interior were "of a better condition." That would have been reason enough for traveling to the west or northwest, but other weights tipped the scale in favor of turning from the coast.

In his *Relacion* Cabeza de Vaca tells how the Indians of the rising plains killed game by setting grass fires, and at this point in the narrative a significant line appears.

The pasturage is taken from the cattle by burning.

That is the first known printed reference to the American bison.

The presence of the buffalo, the most valuable of all wild animals, to the north and west unquestionably was a factor in the selection of a route. Up to this winter, Cabeza de Vaca had eaten of their meat on three occasions, and he thought the taste superior to that of Spanish cows. He set down this meaningful statement about the wild cattle:

"... they come from a northerly direction, ranging through a tract of more than four hundred leagues ..."

Four hundred leagues was more than a thousand miles. If the distance itself was disheartening, it gave rise to thoughts that made the blood of the four men race. Perhaps the land bordered on the great South Sea which Balboa and others had seen! Perhaps the land opened on a strait to India and Japan! Perhaps it was a land richer than Mexico or the islands of the Caribbean!

In the spring of 1535 they left the Avavares and traveled toward the northwest.

VI

THESE were the four men who would be the first to cross North America north of Mexico. They would turn on a great light where only darkness existed. They would prove that the Continent grew wider in the north and was a solid land mass, thereby drastically changing the maps of the Western Hemisphere, which had been drawn only from the imaginations of cartographers.

It was not physical force which won them passage through the unknown, through numerous tribes which did not know that either white or black men existed on the earth. It was the force of faith, not alone faith in their God, but faith in themselves. And it was the force of kindness, the force of indestructible courage, the force of justice.

They had no more than left the Avavares before they

found that their fame as medicine men had preceded them. As they moved across the great high plains of Texas on their epic march they were hailed as gods of the sun by hundreds of Indians who trailed along with them. On occasions, so great was the crush of people about them that their lives were endangered.

In every Indian town they received a tumultuous reception. Men, women and children fought each other to touch them, dancing and leaping in the air "with such yells as were terrific." On across the mesas and deserts, the rivers and hills, which were blank spots on the maps of the world, which no people except the Indians who lived among them had ever seen, on went the savage, colorful parade, a riotous weird pageant which would have no equal in the centuries to come.

Somewhere along the Colorado River of Texas an event took place which would have a great influence on the ultimate fate of Estevanico the Black. This paragraph in the *Relacion* tells of it:

"At sunset we reached a hundred Indian habitations . . . They brought us gourds bored with holes and having pebbles in them, an instrument for the most important occasions, produced only at the dance or to effect cures, and which none dare touch but those who own them. They say there is virtue in them, and because they do not grow in that country, they come from heaven; nor do they know where they are to be found, only that the rivers bring them in their floods."

A few pages later, speaking of other Indians farther along the trail, the *Relacion* contains this entry:

"When we came near the houses all the inhabitants ran out with delight and great festivity to receive us.

Among other things, two of their physicians gave us two gourds, and thenceforth we carried these with us, and added to our authority a token highly reverenced by Indians."

These were the famous medicine rattles of the Southwest, among the holiest of all Indian religious instruments. From time immemorial the Pueblo Indians cultivated gourds, making both rattles and utensils of them. Yet, the four travelers had received them from plains people, who professed not to know their origin . . . they came on the floods of the rivers.

It cannot be authoritatively stated that these particular plains people had any direct contact with the Pueblo Indians of New Mexico, but their trading and hunting expeditions could have taken them westward to the Pecos and the Rio Grande, or, at least, to other tribes whose domains lay along those rivers. There were numerous pueblos on the upper reaches of both the Pecos and the Rio Grande, and the gourds could have come downstream from those communities.

It can be authoritatively stated, however, that Estevanico added at least one of the medicine rattles obtained on the Colorado River of Texas to his personal effects.

For him it was an instrument of death.

That established trade channels did exist to some extent between the tribes of central and west Texas and others far to the west is indicated by this account in the *Relacion:*

"Among the articles given us, Andres Dorantes received a hawk-bell of copper, thick and large, figured with a face, which the natives had shown, greatly prizing it. They told him they had received it from others, their neighbors; we asked them whence the others had obtained it, and they said it had been brought from the northern direction, where there was much copper, which was highly esteemed. We concluded that whencesoever it came there was a foundry, and that work was done in hollow form."

A short time later the hawk-bell was shown to other Indians, and Cabeza de Vaca states:

". . . they told us that in the place whence that had come, were buried many plates of the same material; it was a thing they greatly esteemed, and whence it came from were fixed habitations."

Great new hope filled the four men. Indians did not have foundries, nor (as far as they knew then) fixed habitations!

Either the Indians had been mistaken or had lied about the direction from which the bell had come. Perhaps they did not know. The fact remained that foundries for the molding of metal, and fixed habitations, could mean only one thing. Mexico! Mexico on the South Sea!

With all possible speed the four men pressed toward the setting sun.

Late in the year 1535 they reached the Rio Grande, near the mouth of the Conchos River.

Now the problem of direction one again faced them. The Indians in the caravan had no knowledge of the source of the big river, nor did they know where it went. In making their decision the four men began with the premise that all rivers of the world flowed into the sea. They had only to stand on the bank of the Rio Grande, and note the course of the sun, to determine that it was flowing toward the southeast. Going in that direction it could not reach the sea that purportedly lay somewhere to the northwest, nor could it reach the South Sea that washed the western shores of New Spain. Therefore, it must go to the sea from which they had come.

Other factors in addition to this simple reasoning turned them up the valley of the Rio Grande. It was their conviction, which had no basis in factual knowledge, that they would find people to the northwest who would know of a feasible passage to their goal. The Indians with them said they knew of no such route, indeed, they swore that neither in the north nor in the west were there inhabitants, and that in either direction the country was barren and destitute and impossible to pass through. Long before this, however, the men had learned that Indians would lie in the hope of keeping the famed children of the sun with them.

They turned up the Rio Grande, and after a few days of travel Castillo and Estevanico were sent ahead to scout the country.

In this way it came about that Estevanico was a co-discoverer of the true Pueblo Indians.

He and Castillo reached a pueblo of the Jumanos. "... these habitations were the first seen, having the appearance and structure of houses," says the *Relacion*. "Here Castillo and Estevanico arrived, and, after talking with the Indians, Castillo returned at the end of three days to the spot where he had left us, and brought five or six of the people. He told us he had found fixed dwellings of civilization, that the inhabitants lived on beans and pumpkins, and that he had seen maize. This news the most of anything delighted us, and for it we gave infinite thanks to our Lord.

"Castillo told us the negro was coming with all the population to wait for us in the road not far off. Accordingly we left, and, having traveled a league and a half, we met the negro and the people coming to receive us.

"They gave us beans, many pumpkins, calabashes, blankets of cowhide and other things ... Six leagues from there, as the night set in we arrived at the houses, where great festivities were made over us. We remained one day, and the next set out with these Indians. They took us to the settled habitations of others, who lived upon the same food."*

One regrets Cabeza de Vaca's parsimony in his descriptions of himself and his companions, but from the brief remarks he did make on the subject, and from the writings of contemporaries, some idea of their appearances may be gained. The three Spaniards undoubtedly wore heavy beards, streaked with the dust of the trail and tied with leather thongs. It can be assumed that their clothes consisted of skin breech-clouts and loose jackets, that their bodies were lean, hard, lithe, and deeply burned by years of exposure. Perhaps about their

*Forty-seven years later, in the fall of 1582, Antonio de Espejo and a small company, traveling north from Mexico, reached a pueblo near the confluence of the Conchos and Rio Grande Rivers. Continuing up the Rio Grande, in the next twelve days they came to four more pueblos. Important is this excerpt from Espejo's account:

"These people are all clothed and seem to have some light of our holy faith; for they made signes of God, looking up towards heaven, and call him in their language *Apalito,* and acknowledge him for their Lord, from whose bountiful hand and mercy they confesse they have received their life and being, and these wordly goods. Many of them with their wives and children came unto the friar that he might crosse and blesse them. We demanding of them, from whom they had received that knowledge of God, they answered, from three Christians, & one Negro which passed that way..."

necks crudely carved wooden crosses were suspended on woven animal hairs.

It seems unquestionable that Estevanico was more startling to behold. The color of ebony, he towered above the squat Indians who swarmed about him, his powerful muscles rippled, his white teeth gleamed, and he strode in a regal manner. His great head was adorned with bright feathers.

Estevanico laughed, and he sang, and he danced, reacting to drums in the way of an Indian brave to whom the throaty rhythms were the sweetest and most inspiring music man was capable of producing. He ordered that women — and he saw to it that they were the most comely — be assigned to attend him, and he had an appreciative eye for the supple limbs and full breasts of Indian girls.

The *Relacion* suggests that he was circumspect only under protest. There had been times before the Rio Grande was reached that his brashness with women had brought objections from their spouses, and Cabeza de Vaca had been obliged to remonstrate. On one or two occasions serious trouble had been narrowly averted.

In the mind of Estevanico the privileges of godhood were not restricted by moral considerations. He was no longer a slave, subject to the orders of a master. He was a shaman, a famed medicine man, a child of the sun, and he saw no reason to restrain or conceal the natural urges he possessed. He obeyed Cabeza de Vaca only because he respected, even revered, him, and he understood that Cabeza de Vaca had a capacity for leadership far greater than either himself or the others. Moreover, he wanted to live as much as anyone.

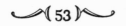

They were a good team, each loyal to himself and to the others. In a physical sense, they were nothing less than supermen. They no longer feared suffering, and they no longer cringed at the prospect of sustained hunger. "We never felt exhaustion," Cabeza de Vaca wrote, "neither were we in fact at all weary, so inured were we to hardship."

It had become Cabeza de Vaca's expressed conviction that unnecessary talk was dangerous, that the role of god was better played in discreet silence. All of them possessed immeasurable influence, and in his estimation this advantage could best be preserved through reservation and detachment. Familiarity and sociability, he believed, would tend to lower them to the level of ordinary men in the eyes of the Indians. Castillo and Dorantes shared this attitude, but Estevanico did not.

The three white men sought to remain aloof, never cold or unfriendly or disdainful but never patronizing or purposefully amiable, and they did not engage in small talk. Estevanico saw no advantage to be gained by silence, and he entered with spirit into the native life as he found it, restraining himself no more than good sense demanded.

"The Negro," said Cabeza de Vaca, "was in constant conversation; he informed himself about the ways we wished to take, of the towns there were, and the matters we desired to know."

Almost invariably . . . except for a few disagreeable scenes which Cabeza de Vaca did not describe . . . Estevanico won favor wherever he went. Perhaps because he was more a child of the night than of the sun, the Indians expected him to be different from his companions. Whether or not this was true, the fact remains that he was welcomed, respected and genuinely liked. Indian women appeared to be more interested in him in some ways than they were in the other strange men who had come among them. The curiosity was mutual... Estevanico was interested in them.

VII

FOR NEARLY three weeks the four men journeyed up the valley of the Rio Grande, until they were within a few miles of the present day city of El Paso. Then they learned of a trail that went toward great mountains in the west, and the Indians said that beyond the mountains was a sea.

It was December, and the Jumanos counseled them not to attempt the crossing in winter. The country to the west was forbidding desert, and few people lived in it.

They had no intention of passing another winter in idleness, and each voted to strike at once directly westward and face whatever dangers awaited them.

They left the Rio Grande near a village known now as San Augustine, about twenty miles south of Ciudad Juarez. The trail ran to the southwest. With a number of Jumanos accompanying them, they set out across the vast desert reaches of Chihuahua.

Desert trails change only when the waterholes along them change, and the trail from San Augustine may still be followed. It took them to the green oasis of Samalayuca. For seventeen days they pressed steadily on, passing through blowing sandhills, passing the salt lake of the Salado, where there were a few sweet water pools, and reached the Santa Maria, where they learned that not all streams have common destiny, the sea. The Santa Maria, a trickle called a river, rose in the desert and flowed some two hundred miles to death in the desert.

Seventeen days to the Santa Maria, and then came seventeen more days of travel toward the west, until one evening as the sun went down, they saw ahead of them the walls of mountains higher than they had ever seen. They had come in sight of the great Sierra Madre.

The weather favored them, and the country grew greener as they climbed, and the little streams became faster and stronger, and there were birds and trees and meadows, and far above them the snow of the peaks glistened against a bright sky.

At last they started down a long valley, and they came once more to villages of permanent dwellings, and there were storage bins filled with maize. These were villages of the Opatas, who belonged to the immense Piman linguistic family.

Everywhere along their route they were most hospitably received. At one banquet they and their followers were offered the hearts of six hundred deer. Cabeza de Vaca named the place Pueblo de los Corazones.* From

*The present town of Ures, Sonora.

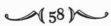

this point onward, Estevanico was among people and traveling through a land he would revisit, and which would be important in the events of his last days on earth.

It was in Pueblo de los Corazones that Cabeza de Vaca was presented with what he thought to be five fine emeralds made into arrowheads. They were probably malachites. Writing of them, he said: "They appeared to be very precious. I asked whence they got these; and they said the stones were brought from some lofty mountains that stand toward the north, where were populous towns and very large houses, and that they were purchased with plumes and the feathers of parrots."

These were the famous towns which would soon come to be known as the Seven Cities of Cibola. The four men had first heard of them from the Jumanos. Now they knew that "emeralds" were to be found in them.

Not only bounteous feasts and fine cotton shawls, but turquoises and other precious stones were given to the visitors by the Opatas. They were also presented with pieces of coral — coral which came from the South Sea! They learned that it was not far distant!

The Opatas led them over the best trail to the south, avoiding the wastelands which they said bordered the great waters. It was on the Yaqui River that the event of which they had dreamed so long took place.

The river was in flood and they were obliged to wait several days for it to recede. During this time hundreds of Indians visited their camp. One day the sharp eyes of Castillo caught sight of a buckle that he knew had come from a sword belt. The buckle was hung on a thong suspended about the neck of a visitor. Stitched to the buckle was a horseshoe nail.

Castillo told Cabeza de Vaca of his discovery. Trembling inwardly with excitement, but endeavoring to display calmness, they examined the buckle and the nail. ". . . we asked the native what they were," said Cabeza de Vaca, "[and] he answered they came from heaven."

It was a reply they might have expected. Very well they understood that in seeking information from an Indian it was usually advisable to proceed casually, perhaps by a circuitous route. A direct approach was impolitic. They had let their excitement carry them off, and they made another attempt:

"We questioned him further, as to who had brought them thence: they all responded that certain men who wore beards like us had come from heaven and arrived at that river, bringing horses, lances and swords, and that they had lanced two Indians.

"In the manner of the utmost indifference we could feign, we asked them what had become of these men. They answered us that they had gone to sea . . ."

Spaniards!

They crossed the Yaqui and hurried on southward, and as they advanced "the news of the Christians continually grew."

It was not all good news. Spanish slave hunters had scourged the country, and sadly Cabeza de Vaca wrote: "We passed through many territories and found them all vacant; their inhabitants wandered fleeing among the mountains, without daring to have houses or till the earth for fear of Christians.

"The sight was one of infinite pain to us, a land very fertile and beautiful, abounding in springs and streams, the hamlets deserted and burned, the people thin and weak, all fleeing or in concealment."

The four men let it be known that they would halt the slave traffic, and the Indians believed them, and shouted with joy, and gave them special presents. "They brought shawls of those they had concealed because of the Christians, presenting them to us," said Cabeza de Vaca, "and they related how the Christians at other times had come through the land, destroying and burning the towns, carrying away half the men, and all the women and the boys."

Amazingly the terrorized people who had suffered so greatly at the hands of other Spaniards received the four men with kindness and respect and seemingly without fear. Cabeza de Vaca understood: "Thence it may at once be seen that, to bring all these people to be Christians and to the obedience of the Imperial Majesty, they must be won by kindness, which is a way certain, and no other is."

It was a lesson Estevanico never forgot.

With more than six hundred Indians surrounding them, they moved on with the greatest possible speed. In the middle of March, 1536, their long search ended.

On the Rio Sinaloa, twenty Spanish horsemen were startled to see a gaunt bearded white man, Cabeza de Vaca, and an immense half-naked Negro, Estevanico, appear out of the bush.

The rest of the journey, over the Camino Real to Mexico City was a triumphal procession. Thousands of people . . . Indians, Spaniards and their bemuddled offspring ... lined the streets of villages and towns to see them pass.

They entered Mexico City on July 24, the day before the Vespers of Saint Iago — the day of St. James the Apostle — and they were carried with cheers along the wide avenues.

"We were," said Cabeza de Vaca, "handsomely treated by the Viceroy and the Marquis del Valle,* and welcomed with joy. They gave us clothing and proffered us whatsoever they had."

The next day a great celebration was held, and there was a jousting of bulls.

*Mendoza and Cortez.

VIII

How well Estevanico was treated in Mexico City, how much he was honored, are questions to which historical records supply no specific answers. Certain reasonable conclusions may be drawn, however, from isolated statements, official actions, and the general trend of events.

The feverish excitement created by the arrival of the four men in the capital was due not so much to their remarkable achievement in surviving, or to their incredible journey, as to the information they brought about the country to the north.

Through all recorded history it will be found that the force which propelled men as they performed great feats of exploration derived more from exhilarating fancies than from known facts. Tenuous but indestructible roots reaching back into improbable realms supplied fire to their blood. Determination came from dreams, and inspiration from legends.

In the summer of 1536 the name of the long lost Seven Cities of Antilia had for generations lingered in the imaginations of those who envisioned themselves reveling in the rewards of successful conquests. It reflected from an ancient tradition, and if they had no evidence of that tradition's authenticity, neither did they have good reasons to disbelieve it.

The old tale was this:

In the Eighth Century, after the Moors had conquered Spain and Portugal, oppressed Christians led by the Archbishop of Oporto and six other bishops sailed westward into the unknown Ocean Sea and discovered the luxurious island of Antilia. Each of the seven bishops founded and ruled a city, and the whole island ... to which the Portuguese gave the appropriate name of *Isla das Sete Citades* ... became a Utopian commonwealth, fabulously rich in gold and jewels and supplied with all manner of food and comforts.

The island was shown on numerous early maps, and although one or more ships reported to have sighted it, it was never found. The name Antilles was given to the West Indian Islands, but that was obviously a misnomer, for neither the descendants of Christians, nor any artifacts indicating that a Portuguese civilization had once existed on them, had been found by Columbus or the conquistadores who followed him.

With all the darkness that remained in the New World, who was to say that the *Isla das Sete Citades* would not some day be rediscovered? Certainly not the ambitious, dreaming, covetous adventurers of New Spain.

The searching and the years moved on apace. Then

suddenly the name of Seven Cities again dominated thoughts and conversations, if not nocturnal hallucinations, in Mexico.

It happened this way:

In May, 1527, Nuno Beltran de Guzman took office as Governor of the Province of Panuco. A few months later he became president of the Audencia, the administrative and judicial board which governed the colony. It was a position which gave him supreme authority, and he used it with wanton disregard for the welfare of his subjects.

Guzman, a personal and political enemy of Cortez, was dishonest, arrogant, and barbarously cruel. Slavery was forbidden by royal decree, but he ignored the law and sold thousands of natives to operators of mines, ranchos and encomiendas throughout the West Indies, pocketing the money paid for them.

The extremities he practiced eventually brought a strong protest from the powerful Bishop Juan de Zumarraga of Mexico. Guzman was commanded to govern his territory with justice and in accordance with colonial statutes.

The reprimand did little good. If Guzman was obliged to curtail his brutal activities to some extent in Panuco, he was not precluded from looking about for other means of gratifying his avarice.

He gazed wonderingly toward the unknown northern interior. What was to be found out there? His hated rival, Cortez, had reached the Pacific, had sent out some ships, and had done some exploring. However, Cortez was in trouble with the courts, he had gone to Spain to defend his rights and his conduct. The northern and western doors stood open.

It was one of his own Indian slaves who greatly influenced Guzman in deciding on a course of action. Pedro de Castaneda told how this happened:*

"In the year 1530 [1529] Nuno de Guzman . . . had in his possession an Indian . . . who was called Tejo by the Spaniards. This Indian said he was the son of a trader who was dead, but that when he was a little boy his father had gone into the back country with fine feathers to trade for ornaments, and that when he came back he brought a large amount of gold and silver, of which there was a good deal in that country. He went with him once or twice, and saw some very large villages, which he compared to Mexico [City] and its environs. He had seen *seven very large towns* which had streets of silver workers. It took forty days to go there from his country, through a wilderness in which nothing grew, except some very small plants about a span high. The way they went was up through the country between the two seas."

Perhaps Tejo had gone with his father to trade with the Pueblo Indians. If he had not, then he knew of their culture and that they lived in permanent towns. This, of course, was common knowledge. Trade between the Pueblos and the tribes of northern Mexico had existed for centuries before the time of Columbus.

Whatever the case, Tejo spoke magic words: *Seven very large towns,* and *gold,* and *streets of silver workers.* If he had not seen these things with his own eyes, he was indeed a clever Indian. He knew what Guzman wanted to hear.

*Castaneda was a chronicler of the Coronado Expedition.

A single question burned in Guzman's mind: Could these be the long lost Seven Cities of Antilia?

He set out to answer it. In regal splendor and with great pageantry, he started from Mexico City late in 1529. Surrounding him was a formidable force of four or five hundred Spaniards and ten thousand Aztecs and Tlascaltecs.

As he rolled onward, Guzman laid waste to the settlements and fields, and inflicted "unspeakable punishment on the native inhabitants."*

His course took him across some of the highest ranges and roughest terrain in Mexico. This route was selected, as Castaneda explained, "so as to get into the region which the Indian [Tejo] said was to be crossed toward the North Sea, in this way getting into the country which they were looking for, which was already named 'The Seven Cities.' He thought, from the forty days of which Tejo had spoken, that it would be found to be about 200 leagues, and that they would easily be able to cross the country."

The opposite was true. The great army broke through to the west coast, but there progress was halted, for they "found the difficulties very great, because the mountain chains which are near the sea are so rough that it was impossible, after great labor, to find a passageway in that region. His whole army had to stay in the district for so long on this account that some rich men who were with him, who had possessions in Mexico, changed their minds, and every day became more anxious to return."

Guzman's quest for the Seven Cities failed, but to secure the lands he conquered on the west coast he

*Hodge, biblio.

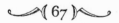

erected a chapel at Tonala, which was the beginning of the city of Guadalajara, and he founded the towns of Santiago de Compostela in Tepic, and San Miguel Culiacan, in Sinaloa. His slave hunters conducted raids as far north as the Yaqui River, where Castillo had seen the Indian wearing a buckle and a nail.

Guzman's political and legal troubles swiftly mounted. He was summoned to appear in Mexico City to stand trial for his violations of the laws and his unauthorized conquests, but he refused to go. In 1533 he was stripped of his title. His friends and supporters began to desert him.

In 1536, three Spaniards and a Negro Moor appeared out of the north. They had come from the land Guzman had hoped to enter. The marvelous tales they told must have made him sick at heart, but there was nothing he could do then. He was through.

Don Antonio Mendoza, the new Viceroy of Mexico, had appointed Francisco Vasquez de Coronado as Guzman's successor. Guzman was arrested, convicted, and, penniless and despised, sent into exile.

But the story of Tejo survived, and in that same year that Guzman was imprisoned, it was given great new meaning by the arrival of Cabeza de Vaca, Castillo, Dorantes and Estevanico. The stirring words brought the name of Seven Cities once more to everyone's lips.

IX

CABEZA DE VACA stated that the Viceroy Mendoza treated him and his companions handsomely and welcomed them with joy. He did not say, as some histories do, that they were house guests of the most powerful man in the New World. There is loose reasoning in such an assumption.

The moment he reached Mexico and came under the rigid rules of its officialdom and its society, Estevanico reverted to his former status as a slave. He enjoyed the freedom and the respect of a colleague during the long journey, but these advantages, or honors, were lost to him, and no longer permitted, once he came within the jurisdiction of the capital court, in which codes, protocol, and status were conscientiously followed. It could hardly have been otherwise.

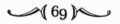

There seems to be no question, however, that Mendoza included Estevanico in at least one or two, and possibly more, audiences he granted to the four men. The Viceroy speaks of the Moor as an intelligent person, as having a special gift for dealing with Indians, and indicated his feeling that Estevanico, having been "everywhere" with the brilliant and competent Cabeza de Vaca, would be most valuable not only in the work of bringing justice and order to the northern frontier but in whatever plans developed for exploring and expanding Spain's dominion.

And from the time he heard of the inconceivable exploits of the four men, and listened to the exciting information they brought of the north, needless to say, great plans began to take shape in Mendoza's thoughts.

Estevanico was well treated, wherever he might have been quartered, and with good reason. Mendoza fully realized his usefulness.

Cabeza de Vaca was a guest in the Viceroy's palace. This honor may have been extended to him because he was the ranking officer of the explorers. More likely it came about because he had been treasurer and provost-marshal of the Narvaez Expedition, posts which had been awarded to him by order of the Spanish Court. Some of his ancesters had distinguished themselves in the King's service, and had won royal appointments, but he was not of the nobility. Indeed, the name Cabeza de Vaca, of which he was very proud, was originally bestowed upon a peasant herdsman on his mother's side of the family.

Mendoza had been sent out to restore royal authority in Spain's New World provinces, in much of which law and order had broken down under violence and because of illegal activities of swashbucklers and other types of reckless adventurers. He had been ordered to end Indian slavery, and to remove conquistadores and officials whose practices and machinations might prove to be inimical to the best interests of the Crown. The southern boundary of the vast territory over which Mendoza ruled could be defined. It was the Isthmus of Panama. The northern boundary was necessarily vague, but considerable light was thrown on its possible extent by the arrival of the four men.

Mendoza lived in a manner befitting his exalted office. "Sixty Indian servants were always in attendance on him and his guests in his palace," wrote Aiton.* "From thirty to forty gentlemen, foot and horse, composed a bodyguard which was always about him, and formed an escort . . ."

Cabeza de Vaca might well have been ill at ease in such an environment, if he had not been a gentleman. Whether Castillo or Dorantes had such an uncomfortable feeling, is not ascertainable. Judged by normal standards, they, too, were gentlemen. There is evidence to show, however, that they were in no way treated indifferently or neglected, nor were they less respected and rewarded than Cabeza de Vaca. Wherever they were housed, in the palace or in some luxurious household, they enjoyed special privileges and remained in the favor of the Viceroy.

There is nothing in historical records to substantiate a contention that any of the four men lied, told fanciful

*See biblio.

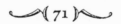

tales, or even exaggerated, about the northern country.*
Certainly Cabeza de Vaca, the chief spokesman, made
no claims about having discovered a fabulously rich
land. It would not have been in character for him to
have uttered statements which were not conservative or
truthful. His *Relacion* supports this assertion.

When repeating stories heard from Indians, he had
not failed to remind his listeners that they were told to
him in several tongues, or in the sign language, and that
he could not vouch for their accuracy. He pointed out
that under such circumstances the margin for error
was great.

No official record states that any of the four men
claimed to have factual knowledge of large cities, or
that they had seen streets of silver workers, found gold
or silver mines, or met people who ate from golden
dishes and adorned themselves with priceless jewels.
They had heard of these things, just as everyone in
Mexico had heard of them, but they had not seen them.

They had, however, seen some things which were
worthy of note, and which might well indicate that the
northern country contained valuable resources. They
had seen people who lived in permanent houses in
fertile valleys, who had maize and other wholesome
foods. They had seen cotton blankets of good quality.
They had spoken with people who *said* bird plumes
were traded for turquoise and wild cattle robes in very
large villages far to the north.

The four men had seen *signs* of gold, antimony, iron,

*Early accounts mention that Cabeza de Vaca and Dorantes collaborated on a
report and a map for Mendoza, and maintain that he sent them to Spain. If
true, neither has been found.

copper and other metals, but the only evidence they themselves had that the country contained any mineral resources consisted of some scoria of iron, some small bags of mica, some galena with which the natives painted their bodies, some turquoise, five "emerald" arrow heads, and a copper bell, which unquestionably had been transported northward from Mexico.

Actually, it did not matter what the four men said. It did not matter whether they were truthful or had let their imaginations run wild. Like a fire in dry prairie grass word spread that they had seen the Seven Cities, that if they had had any means of carrying it they would have returned with an inconceivably large fortune. Throughout the capital men claimed that they had heard them tell of crossing streams which flowed in beds of gold, of seeing Indian children playing with diamonds, pearls and emeralds which had been cast away as worthless, of having passed hills of silver and at least one mountain which contained so many jewels of all kinds that one dared not look at in the sunlight for fear of being blinded.

The Viceroy Mendoza was intrigued, perhaps fascinated but he was not blinded by either an unfounded rumor of a mountain of jewels or by his own illusions. Indeed, his eyes were wide open, and what they saw was not all pleasant or encouraging.

He had been in Mexico only a year, and he was uneasy in the face of the many problems confronting him. He would have liked nothing better than to discover new lands and take possession of them for the Crown, but he had no intention of rushing into expensive conquests without adequate preparation or without some assurance that he had a reasonable chance of succeeding.

Mendoza moved cautiously, but he did move. When he concluded that an investigation of the north would be advisable, he, quite naturally, suggested that Cabeza de Vaca head an exploring party. There was no one better for such a task.

Cabeza de Vaca declined. At the moment he was far more interested in going home, in a reunion with his wife, in sitting in a Jerez de la Frontera patio that was bathed in the soft blue light of late afternoon. Those were the riches he desired the most . . . at least, that is what he led persons to believe. It turned out later, after he had reached Spain, that he also had some thoughts as to his future.

It would be disclosed that Cabeza de Vaca and Dorantes had formulated a plan, necessarily vague at the time, to undertake another expedition to northern North America. In Spain, Cabeza de Vaca petitioned the Royal Court for a commission as Governor of Florida. He was too late. The post had already been awarded to a conquistadore named Hernando de Soto.

Thus, whatever plan Cabeza de Vaca and Dorantes had made was defeated.

Chronicles of the day relate that Dorantes, preparing to go home, gave to Mendoza one of his most valuable and highly esteemed possessions as a gesture of friendship . . . Estevanico. Well might one question the accuracy of that report. The shrewd Mendoza fully appreciated Estevanico's ability and the value of the Moor's training and experience under Cabeza de Vaca. It would not be strange if he requested that Estevanico be placed in his service. Dorantes would have been in no position to refuse such a request.

Whatever the truth about Estevanico, Dorantes was in Vera Cruz in the spring of 1537, waiting to sail for Spain, when he received a message from Mendoza asking him to return to Mexico City. He went back, and the Viceroy asked him to lead a small expedition to the north to find out what really was there.

Dorantes was in a somewhat awkward position. It was a commission he was unable to reject.

Mendoza looked upon the plan as being in keeping with the cautious action he desired. He appropriated some money, men and supplies . . . a few soldiers, friars and slaves . . . for the undertaking, reporting to the Emperor an estimated cost of four thousand pesos, a sum he considered modest and well worth the gamble.

Then Dorantes got up enough nerve to announce that he had changed his mind, and did not care to go.

Meanwhile, Castillo had chosen to remain in Mexico. He had become enamored of a wealthy widow, and Mendoza had rewarded him with half the income of the Indian lands of Tehuacan. The future looked bright to Castillo, and Mexico was a very pleasant land.*

Angered by the setback in his plans, Mendoza wrote the Emperor: "Andres Dorantes, one of those comprising the army of Panphilo de Narvaez, has come to me, and I have had frequent conferences with him, thinking he might render a great service to your Majesty if I should send him with forty or forty-five horsemen and all the things necessary to explore that country. I have

*The Castillos lived quietly and unostentatiously in Mexico City. They had no sons, but Señora Castillo gave birth to eleven daughters.

spent a great amount of silver for the expedition, but for reasons unknown to me the affair has come to naught. From all the preparations I have made there are left to me only a Negro who came with Dorantes, some slaves whom I have purchased, and some Indians, natives of the country, whom I have assembled."

Dorantes's change of heart may have been a mystery to Mendoza, but there seemed to be no doubt that it was clear to Dorantes himself. In going off to the north in command of an expedition, he would have been disloyal to his old comrade, Cabeza de Vaca. They had an agreement, and Cabeza de Vaca had gone to Spain with the intention of fulfilling it. Dorantes could not have known then that it could not be fulfilled.

Mendoza was put out with Dorantes, but his anger did not long endure. Like Castillo, Dorantes now decided to remain in Mexico. He, too, married a wealthy widow, Marie de la Torre. She owned extensive properties and received large rents in the towns of Asala and Jalazinto. And like the Castillos, the Dorantes had eleven children. Restored to the Viceroy's favor, Dorantes served as an officer in the conquest of Jalisco. He lived for many years, a man of affluence, respect and position.

". . . there are left to me only a Negro . . . some slaves . . . and some Indians . . ."

Of the four men who had seen the north country, only Estevanico remained to lead Mendoza's projected expedition. And that could not be done. A Negro slave, regardless of his ability and experience, could not be placed in command of an expedition, whatever its nature. If Indians would serve him loyally, Spanish soldiers would resent his authority, and not only might refuse to obey him in the wilderness but might well dispose of him with a timely shot in the back.

Mendoza struggled with his problem, but fate solved it for him.

It happened that there appeared in Mexico City at precisely the right moment one Fray Marcos de Niza.*

For seven years, displaying a craving for adventure and sightseeing which challenged his love for his work as a missionary, Fray Marcos had galivanted about the New World. He had reached Santo Domingo in 1531, soon went on to Guatemala, then traveled with Alvarado to South America. He was with Pizarro in Peru and witnessed the conquests and the destruction of both that country and Ecuador. In 1536, he returned to Guatemala. There he took pen in hand and wrote Bishop Zumarraga of Mexico about the atrocities he had seen. Zumarraga asked him to come to the capital, and he reached it early in 1537.

When he heard Fray Marcos's complete story of the cruelties inflicted on the people of South America, the Bishop ordered him to prepare a written account. Fray Marcos obeyed, and copies were sent to Spain. Fray Marcos also was presented to Mendoza, who was as shocked by the narrative as Zumarraga.

Fray Marcos and another padre, Fray Onarato, were sent off to western Mexico to carry on their missionary duties, but Mendoza already had other plans for them.

Fray Marcos was just the man the Viceroy wanted. The friar's qualifications were outstanding, his recommendations unqualified and glowing. He had not been long in Mexico before both Mendoza and Zumarraga

*He was so designated because he had lived for some time at Nice.

understood that he was a man of great imagination, physically strong, brimming with ardor and optimism. The Bishop spoke of him as "reliable, of approved virtue and fine religious zeal." Mendoza said of him that he was "habituated to hardships, experienced in the affairs of the Indies, conscientious, and of exemplary conduct." The Franciscan Provincial in Mexico, Fray Ciudad-Rodrigo, added the testimonial that Marcos was "skilled in cosmography and in the arts of the sea, as well as in theology."

It may be wondered how well, if at all, the Viceroy understood that inseparably linked with Fray Marcos's imagination, ardor, optimism, zeal and enthusiasm were two other pronounced qualities: talent as a promoter and the ability to dramatize himself and everything he did. Perhaps Mendoza was astute enough to recognize that he possessed such gifts. If he did not, he soon became fully and unhappily aware of it.

Mendoza wrote to the Emperor for permission to send Fray Marcos on a scouting expedition to the north. Approval of the plan reached Mexico from Charles V in the late summer of 1538. Mendoza immediately took action. At the time, Fray Marcos happened to be back from the west, and in the capital, and in September he was named to head the northern venture. With him would go his companion, Fray Onarato, and some Indian slaves. Their guide would be Estevanico.

Things were shaping up to Mendoza's satisfaction. As no professional soldiers would go along, no one would have to be paid, and the cost of equipment and supplies would be small. Mendoza would not have to endanger his own record with expenditures of the King's money on a scheme he was not fully convinced would turn out to be profitable.

The plan was benefitted by an event of importance. In August of 1538, Mendoza had appointed a young nobleman, only twenty-eight years of age, Governor of Nueva Galicia. He was Don Francisco Vasquez de Coronado.

Coronado had come to Mexico as a gentleman member of Mendoza's staff. The Viceroy held him in high esteem, and considered him competent and loyal. Inasmuch as the investigation of the north must emanate from the west coast province of Nueva Galicia, and Coronado would be there as governor, Mendoza instructed him to supervise preparations for it. It was not an obligation unwelcome to Coronado. On the contrary, his own dreams of conquest and riches for both his country and himself were no less fervid than those of Mendoza, or, for that matter, anyone else.

Assisting the two friars and Estevanico in getting underway, however, was not the only pressing responsibility placed upon Coronado's youthful shoulders. There was trouble in Culiacan, where settlers were abusing Indians, and an uprising appeared to be imminent. Also, reports that gold had been discovered in Topia had reached the capital. These areas were within Coronado's jurisdiction, and he was ordered to quell any Indian revolt in the making, investigate the reports from Topia, and secure the fealty of the natives by halting all slave-taking and assuring them of the Viceroy's protection. Quite a job for a young man of twenty-eight, but Coronado soon demonstrated that he was equal to it.

X

IN THE FALL OF 1538 a brilliant procession of gentleman adventurers, led by the new governor of Nueva Galicia, made its way along the high rocky road that ran out of the valley of Mexico to Guadalajara, Compostela and the Pacific coast. In the wake of the column traveled a group which in appearance contrasted dramatically with the splendor and ostentation of Coronado and his military escort.

No armor glistened in the sun, no plumes or banners waved, in the little company for which Estevanico was the pathfinder. With him paddled the sandled friars, Marcos and Onarato, clad in robes of dusty Zaragosa cloth, and a score of half-naked Indians charged with the personal bundles and the few articles of equipment which would go with them on their journey into the unknown.

The Viceroy's written instructions to Fray Marcos regarding the objectives and the conduct of the mission were handed to the friar by Coronado. They were detailed and exhaustive, and no doubt had been prepared with the intention of impressing the King as much as the missionary.

"Upon arriving at the province of Culiacan," Mendoza told Marcos, "you are to exhort and urge the Spaniards residing in the town of San Miguel [de Culiacan] to treat the peaceful Indians well and not to employ them in excessive tasks, assuring them that by so doing they will be granted favors and rewards by his Majesty for the hardships they have endured there, and that they will find in me a good supporter for their claims. If they do the opposite they will incur punishment and disfavor."

The following order involved diplomatic work that might well have been entrusted to Estevanico, whose ability as an envoy to the Indians Mendoza fully appreciated, but such an arrangement was not possible. Fray Marcos was the designated head of the company. Yet, the Viceroy could have held no doubts about Marcos passing on the instructions to the accomplished Moor, with the result that the desired end would be achieved.

The matter of dealing with the natives was important to Mendoza, and he dwelt at length on it, telling Marcos:

"You shall make clear to the Indians that I am sending you in the name of his Majesty to tell them that the Spaniards shall treat them well, to let them know that he regrets the abuses and harm they have suffered, and that from now on they shall be well treated and those who may mistreat them shall be punished."

It was a message very similar in content to that delivered to the Indians by Cabeza de Vaca and Estevanico, when they had pledged themselves to do all in their power to halt the cruelties inflicted by Guzman. This passage from the *Relacion*, recounting the advice sent to the Indians who had fled their homes in terror from the slave hunters, may be recalled:

"We ordered them to come down from the mountains in confidence and peace, inhabit the whole country and construct their houses: among these they should build one for God . . . and, when Christians came among them, they should go out to receive them with crosses in their hands, without bows or any arms . . . and the Christians would do them no injury, but be their friends . . ."

It was almost as if Mendoza were repeating the words of the *Relacion*. "Likewise," he told Marcos, "you are to assure them that no more slaves shall be taken from among them and that they are not to be taken away from their lands: on the contrary, they shall be left alone as free people, without suffering any harm. Tell them that they should not be afraid, but acknowledge God, our Lord, Who is in heaven, and the emperor, as he has been placed on earth by His hand to rule and govern it."

Now Mendoza suggested that Marcos might do a little private reporting regarding the attitude and activities of Coronado in relation to the Indian question. He told the friar: "Since Francisco Vasquez de Coronado, whom his Majesty has appointed governor of that province, will go with you as far as the town of San Miguel de Culiacan, you shall inform me of how he provides for the affairs of that town in matters pertaining to the service of God, our Lord, and the conversion and good treatment of the natives of that province."

If Coronado didn't like the possibilities inherent in that order, there was nothing he could do about it, except be careful.

At last Mendoza got down to the business of the northern mission, telling Marcos: "If with the aid of God our Lord and the grace of the Holy Spirit you should find a way to go on and penetrate the land in the interior, you shall take along Esteban de Dorantes as guide."

The designation prompts questions. Did Mendoza own Estevanico? Had he only borrowed him? Had Dorantes declined to give away his loyal servant and good companion?

The answers are not available, but, one way or another, Mendoza had secured the services of the man he considered the most valuable for the purposes in mind.

Mendoza commanded that Estevanico obey Fray Marcos in whatever the friar "may order him, as he would obey me in person." If Estevanico should fail to do so, "he will be at fault and incur the penalties falling on those who disobey the persons empowered by his Majesty to command them." This was strong talk in such a commonplace issue as a slave's obedience. Slaves were not in the habit of being disobedient, and it did not ordinarily take a threat in the name of the King of Spain to impress upon them the need for toeing the line.

In view of what occurred later on the northern trail, the order takes on a special meaning.

Once again words of Cabeza de Vaca are recalled. They appear in the *Relacion*, which had not yet been printed in the fall of 1538, but they may have been spoken to the Viceroy, or they may have been in the report Cabeza de Vaca wrote for him, and which has never come to light. They were: ". . . it may at once be seen that, to bring all these people to be Christians and to the obedience of the Imperial Majesty, they must be won by kindness, which is a way certain, and no other is."

Mendoza admonished Fray Marcos to travel the safest way possible, and before entering an area to learn whether the natives in it were at war or at peace among themselves. This was to be done so that Indians "may not do any violence to your person" which would necessitate reprisals against them. Such an unfortunate event, thought Mendoza, instead of helping and enlightening them, "would do just the opposite." He wanted nothing to happen which would force him to deviate from a program of kindness.

The Viceroy was very specific in telling the friar what to look for, and what intelligence to send back, saying: "You shall be very careful to observe the number of people that there are, whether they are few or many, and whether they are scattered or living together. Note also the nature, fertility and climate of the land; the trees, plants and domestic and wild animals there may be; the character of the country, whether it is broken or flat; the rivers, whether they are large or small; the stones and metals which there are; and of all things that be sent or brought, send or bring samples of them in order that his majesty may be informed of everything."

It was not only His Majesty whom Mendoza wished to inform. He was sticking his own neck out on what might turn out to be an unfortunate undertaking, and he wanted to give himself all the protection he could. What His Majesty never knew would not hurt him.

Mendoza apparently could not dislodge from his mind the popular conception of northern North America as two narrow isthmuses between two oceans. Cabeza de Vaca and his companions had shown the belief to be erroneous, but European mapmakers had not yet had an opportunity to study their reports, and, besides, Mendoza was a person who was always suspicious of information he had not confirmed himself. If he had no reason to doubt the statements of Cabeza de Vaca and Dorantes, nor to suspect the accuracy of the map they purportedly prepared for him, he would not be satisfied until he had additional proof that they were correct. After all, that was the chief purpose of the reconnaissance . . . to check on the reports of the four men.

Thus, Mendoza reminded Fray Marcos that he was to "endeavor always to learn if there is any information about the seacoast, both of the North and South Seas, for it may be that the land narrows and that a sea inlet reaches the interior of the land. If you should reach the coast of the South Sea (?), leave letters buried at the headlands, at the foot of some tree outstanding for its size, telling of what you think should be known. Mark the tree with a cross where the letters are left, so that they may be found. Likewise, at the mouths of rivers and suitable harbors, on prominent trees near the water, make the same sign, a cross, and leave letters. Thus if I send ships they will be advised to look for this sign."

A thorough man, Mendoza. Moreover, he already was thinking about sending a sea expedition to the north. He had great hopes.

"Try always to send reports through Indians, telling how you are faring, how you are received, and particularly what you may find," he went on to Marcos.

"If God our Lord should will it that you find some large settlement which you think would be a good place for establishing a monastery and for sending friars who would devote themselves to conversions, you are to send a report by Indians, or return yourself, to Culiacan. Send back reports with the utmost secrecy so that appropriate steps may be taken without disturbing anything, because in the pacification of what is discovered the services of our Lord and the welfare of the natives shall be taken into consideration."

Serving the Lord and protecting the natives were handy reasons for secrecy, until the value of the discoveries, such as gold mines and mountains of jewels, could be thoroughly assayed and secured.

Of course, the whole land belonged to the Lord, but Marcos, nevertheless, was to take possession of it for His Majesty, the King of Spain, in the name of Mendoza. ". . . set up markers that you feel are required for this purpose," the Viceroy commanded Fray Marcos.

Compostela was reached in December, and as the year of 1539 began, Coronado and his soldiers, and Fray Marcos, Fray Onorato, Estevanico, and their Indians, were moving along the jungle trail to Culiacan. Coronado made a point of writing to Mendoza that Fray Marcos was being enthusiastically welcomed by the natives along the way. While this was true, there was a great deal more that might have been said about the situation.

In his instructions to Marcos, Mendoza made this statement: "Likewise the said governor Francisco Vasquez is taking along the Indians who came with Dorantes and others from these regions who could be brought together, so that if he and you consider it advisable that some of them should go along, you may employ them in the service of our Lord as you deem fitting."

Indians who had come with Dorantes, and, therefore, with Estevanico, were in the caravan to Culiacan. Even more important, Estevanico himself was there. No better emissaries for Fray Marcos could have been found. The people saw the Indians coming back unharmed to their homelands, and the respected and trusted black man was leading them. They brought good news, assurances of protection, and the end of slavery and other cruelties. The natives along the route had never heard of Fray Marcos, but if he was a companion and friend of Estevanico and the Indians who had gone to Mexico City, that was good enough for them. It would have been strange, indeed, if Fray Marcos had not been cordially welcomed.

Winter passed at Culiacan, and the spring of 1539 was in full glory along the Pacific coast when the little group turned northward on their great adventure.

XI

NATIVE SCOUTS had been sent ahead some distance from Culiacan to announce the expedition and to observe conditions. This was in keeping with Mendoza's orders. The scouts reported that the tribes were peaceful, and that the visitors would be hospitably received and assisted. A number of Indians who had known Cabeza de Vaca, Dorantes, Castillo and Estevanico came from Petatlan and El Cuchillo to escort the company to their respective homes.

"When the journey of exploration was thus assured," Coronado wrote Mendoza, "Fray Marcos, his friend [Onorato], the Negro, and other slaves and Indians whom I had given them departed, after twelve days devoted to their preparations."

It was on Friday, March 7, 1539, that the start was

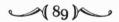

made. Strange and colorful contrasts were portrayed by the members of the group, all of whom were on foot . . . the naked coppery Indians, the two friars in their sober gray habits, and, at the head of all, Estevanico the Black.

As far as Pueblo de los Corazones the trail would hug the foot of the towering Sierra Madre, winding through lush valleys, rugged foothills, and deep canyons, never far from the sea until it swung inland at the northern end of the great Mexican range and ran on into the vast deserts that barred the way to the unknown.

"I command him to obey you . . ." Mendoza had written of Estevanico to Fray Marcos.

Estevanico had no intention of obeying anyone. He fully realized that once they were in the wilderness, beyond the reach of the military, the friars would be completely dependent upon him for their survival. He would be the one who would make decisions, and there is no reason to think that he did not relish the idea of being in such an influential position.

If his audiences with Mendoza and the attention and respect paid to him in the capital had greatly inflated his ego, it would not have been an unusual reaction. What other slave had been given such consideration, and called *intelligent,* by a Viceroy?

If he was not in name commander of the mission, he was in fact. He had been over the trail as far as Pueblo de los Corazones. He was the man the Indians knew, and their faith would be in him. No longer would he be only an assistant medicine man overshadowed by the great Cabeza de Vaca. Now he would be a god in his own right.

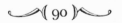

In preparing for the journey, Estevanico had acquired considerable personal baggage, clothing and ornaments, a shelter tent and sleeping robes . . . accouterments he deemed no more than proper for a personage of his high station . . . and these things and the simpler effects of the friars were borne on the backs of slaves. It must have been extremely gratifying to him to think of himself, not as a slave, not as a servant, but as a guide with slaves and servants to answer his beck and call.

He also had come into possession, by what means is not clear, of two greyhounds, and the noble animals trotted obediently beside him.

In one of his packs was a medicine rattle, one of those acquired from the Indians in west Texas. The story of his life might well have had a different ending, and the history of the Southwest might have been very different, if the gourd had been left in Mexico City.

Estevanico had adorned himself in a manner he considered suitable for the occasion. His powerful legs and arms were decorated with clusters of bright feathers. A crown of plumes accentuated his height. Little bells tinkled merrily on his ankles. Turquoise and pieces of coral, presented to him by Indians along the way, were strung on thongs and dripped over his big chest.

He soon acquired a harem, Indian girls he found especially pleasing, and they straggled along in his wake, much to the consternation and disapproval of the padres.

Among the personal possessions Estevanico prized highly were four large dinner plates. They comprised his *servicio de mesa*. On them he was ceremoniously served each meal, and he permitted no one else to use them. His food was specifically prepared for him, and consisted of the finest delicacies his retinue was able to obtain.

The first serious setback of the expedition occurred at Petatlan on the Sinaloa River. Fray Onorato was taken ill. After a wait of three days it became apparent that he would be unable to continue. Fray Marcos ordered that he be carried back to Culiacan, a distance of some sixty leagues, on a litter.*

Bidding a sad farewell to his old companion, Fray Marcos, "guided by the Holy Spirit" — and also by Estevanico — resumed the journey.

Fray Marcos was honored as an emissary of the all-powerful white God by the Indians, but Estevanico received the greater attention, and was in reality more esteemed and revered. This was not alone because the natives had seen him before and knew he was a true friend.

Contrary to popular belief, Indians love fun, jokes, clever pantomime, revelry and story-telling. They appreciated Estevanico's gaiety, his willingness to join them in religious ceremonials and social festivities, and they were drawn to him by his forceful and dominating personality.

Fray Marcos wrote that after leaving Petatlan "I continued on my way for some twenty-five or thirty leagues ..." and "... some Indians from the island visited by the Marques del Valle [Cortez] came to see me. From them assured myself that it is an island and not the mainland, as some claim." If the Indians had come from Cortez's Island of Pearls, they had come a long way,

*Fray Onorato recovered and resumed his duties in Compostela.

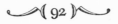

indeed — clear across the Sea of Cortez, which would come to be known as the Gulf of California. More likely they had come only from the coast, or perhaps from some island just off it.

In a pouch Fray Marcos carried a few pieces of gold and silver, pearls and other precious stones. He had been instructed to take these with him to show to Indians in the hope they would direct him to valuables of the same kinds. The Indians from the islands knew of pearls, but they had none, or so they said.

When the Rio Fuertes was reached, Fray Marcos reported that he met other Indians "who marveled at seeing me, because they knew nothing of Christians." Something is amiss in that statement, for Spanish slave hunters had for several years conducted raids north of this place, and, three years before, Cabeza de Vaca and his companions had passed through the area. It seems doubtful that an Indian existed who did not know of their journey.

In any case, Fray Marcos indicated that he was dutifully following orders. He said: "I tried by all possible means to learn about a country with many settlements and with people more advanced and cultured than those I had met. They told me that four or five days inland, where the cordilleras of the sierras end, there is an open valley in which they said were many large settlements and people clothed in cotton."

When Fray Marcos showed them his gold samples, these Indians informed him "there were vessels of it among the people of the valley, and that they wore round articles of that gold hanging from their noses and ears and that they have some small blades made of it, with which they scrape and remove their sweat."

The open valley, or *abra*, was the valley of the Rio Mayo. If the people living in it were as rich as Fray Marcos's Indian informers made out, why didn't he visit them? Certainly Mendoza would have been pleased with such a discovery. He undoubtedly didn't go because Estevanico, the competent interpreter and sign language expert, told him the Indians were pulling his leg, or simply trying to please him by telling him what they knew he wanted to hear. Estevanico was not to be fooled by tall tales.

The mission went on. Vacapa, in the present State of Sinaloa, was reached on March 21, two days before Passion Sunday.

It was there that Fray Marcos made the decision which so drastically changed the nature of the expedition, and which set the course that led to its tragic conclusion.

Planning to remain in Vacapa until after Easter, he sent Estevanico on ahead.

Up to this point, Fray Marcos could not truthfully have said that his journey had not been successful beyond all expectations.* Indeed, it had been nothing less than a triumphal march. At times hundreds of people had crowded about Fray Marcos and Estevanico, pleading to hear about the great God in Heaven, beseeching them to cure ills with a touch of their hands, to assure them happiness and protection with a sign of the cross.

Fray Marcos reported simply that he had sent Este-

*Coronado had written Mendoza that if the Indians had received the friar "only one-tenth as warmly it would have been more than enough."

vanico ahead "to see whether, by that route, information could be obtained of what we were seeking." The
explanation is notable more for its omissions than for
its completeness.

The truth was that he had become deeply disturbed
by the actions of his guide, by Estevanico's conduct and
attitude. Despite his strongly expressed disapproval,
Estevanico swaggered through medicine ceremonies,
made the sign of the cross over the sick, and performed
religious rites. He ignored Fray Marcos's demand that
he reject the women offered him. He saw no reason to
refuse the turquoise and coral and feathers and count-
less other gifts proffered by his hosts. In fact, he had no
hesitancy in asking for any article which attracted his
eye, and his acquisitions were, in Fray Marcos's view,
reaching vulgar proportions.

Castaneda had his own opinion of the situation. He
plainly states that "the negro did not get on well with
the friars, because he took the women that were given
him and collected turquoises, and got together a stock
of everything. Besides, the Indians in those places
through which they went got along with the negro better, because they had seen him before. This was the
reason he was sent on ahead to open up the way and
pacify the Indians, so that when the others came along
they had nothing to do except to keep an account of the
things for which they were looking."

It wasn't quite that simple. In all honesty, Fray Marcos could not have denied that Estevanico for the most
part was doing an excellent job. For a time he had har-
bored the hope that his guide would grow weary of
carousing, dancing half the night and drinking the vile

native stimulants. Apparently he had become convinced that was not to happen, and had begun to fear that serious difficulties might arise. After all, there was a mission to be carried out for the Viceroy, as well as for the Church, and one had to consider that above all else.

Fray Marcos, at last, had concluded that the entire venture might be better served . . . at least he would be less embarrassed and discord would be avoided . . . if he let the irrepressible Moor go on ahead. If Estevanico got into serious trouble, it might be just as well to let him get out as best he could by himself.

Fray Marcos gave Estevanico orders. He was to advance no more than fifty or sixty leagues. "I arranged with him," he reported, "that should he learn of some inhabited and rich country — something really important — he should not go any farther but return in person or send me Indians bearing the following sign: If it were something moderate, he should send me a white cross a span in size; if it were of greater importance, he should send me one two spans in size; and if it were something greater and better than New Spain, he should send me a large cross."

Estevanico the Black set out on the journey that would win for him an outstanding place in the history of American exploration . . . on the trail to his destiny.

XII

It was a wild and beautiful procession that wound its way northward under the morning shadows of the impregnable Sierra Madre. At the head of the column Estevanico, with his greyhounds and his tinkling bells and turquoises and feathers and corals, strode in a regal manner. Always near him was Bartolome, a young native of Petalan, who was his chief aide. Behind them trailed some three hundred Indians.

Estevanico adopted a practice that had been successfully used by Cabeza de Vaca. Each day he sent ahead Indian runners to announce his coming. They carried with them the sacred gourd rattle.

Fray Marcos rested at Vacapa and made his Easter devotions. He was completely astonished when Indian messengers arrived with a cross the size of a man. Estevanico had been gone then only four days.

Even more amazing was the information the messengers brought. Estevanico had instructed them to tell the padre that he "had met people who informed him of the greatest thing in the world," great cities!

Estevanico had Indians with him who had seen them, and one of the messengers himself had been to them.

"This person," said Fray Marcos, "told me so many marvels of the land that I postponed believing them until after seeing them or having further verification. He told me that it was thirty days travel from the place where Esteban was to the first city of the land, which is called Cibola."

If the name of Cibola had been previously known to the Spaniards in Mexico, no documentary proof of the fact has been discovered. This is believed to be the first time the name was used in connection with the Seven Cities.

"He [the courier]," Fray Marcos wrote, "says that in the first province there are seven very large cities, all under one ruler, with large houses of stone and lime, all joined in an orderly manner, and the ruler's house is four stories high. The doors have many decorations of turquoises, of which there is a great abundance, and the people are very well clothed. There are other provinces farther on, each one of which he claims to be much more important than these seven cities. I rendered thanks to our Lord."

If information about the pueblos was news to Fray Marcos, it was not to anyone else in the expedition. One has no way of knowing, of course, what the messenger actually told him, or how much of the story he understood.

Also, Estevanico had developed plans and ideas of his own, and they must be taken into consideration. Descriptions of the pueblos were not new to him. He had heard them several years before, the first time on the Rio Grande. He had heard them from the Opatas in the Valle de Sonora and at Pueblo de los Corazones, and probably from other Indians in Mexico. Now he had heard them again. He was fully aware that trade was carried on between the dwellers of the cities and tribes far to the south, and he had seen evidence of that trade in buffalo robes, cotton garments, and various kinds of stones.

Estevanico knew what he was doing, and he knew what he intended to do.

Eager as he was to go forward, Fray Marcos remained at Vacapa until runners he had dispatched to the sea coast had returned. He had sent them to bring back coastal Indians from whom he hoped to obtain information about the country, and they had succeeded in the mission. The Indians from the Gulf of California wore shell decorations of a kind that contained pearls, told of people who dwelt on islands and traveled on rafts, and presented him with large shields made of hides which were so tough that he did not believe they could be pierced by a crossbow.

Fray Marcos was almost ready to leave Vacapa when more couriers arrived from Estevanico. They brought a cross as large as the previous one, and a message to the friar to hurry northward. About the same time he was visited by several natives from the northeast who confirmed the story of the Seven Cities.

In a state of high excitement, Fray Marcos set out

from Vacapa two days after Easter Sunday. On either April 10th or 11th, he reached the Indian village from which Estevanico had sent the first cross, and where he had promised to wait.

Estevanico had gone on.

This was the beginning of one of the strangest and most notable chases in American history.

If he was disappointed to find that Estevanico had not kept his word, Fray Marcos was cheered by the information the villagers gave him: "They advised me that besides these seven cities there were three other kingdoms called Marata, Acus and Totonteac. They gave me some hides of cattle so well tanned and worked that they looked as if they had been made by men of higher culture. The natives all said that the hides came from Cibola."

The next day Fray Marcos went on and "came to a settlement where Esteban Dorantes had left a large cross as proof that the information about the good country was always increasing."

Estevanico also had left word for his commander that he would wait at a place he described as "the edge of the first despoblado."*

Fray Marcos did not forget his orders from Mendoza. Near Conicari he erected two crosses "and took possession in accordance with the instructions, because this seemed to me a better country than the one we had left behind, and it seemed proper to institute acts of possession from here on."

Then he went ahead as fast as he could travel, hoping to catch up with the disobedient Estevanico. For five

*Desolate area.

days he continued, in each village learning to his aggravation that the Moor had departed.

Castaneda would make the flat charge that Estevanico kept ahead of Fray Marcos because he "thought he could get all the reputation and honor himself, and that if alone he should discover those settlements with such famous high houses, he would be considered bold and courageous."

That is undoubtedly true, but more should be said about the matter. Estevanico was greedy. He wanted not only wealth but honor and fame and recognition. It was his belief that he could gain them by being the discoverer of the Seven Cities of Cibola.

Yet, he was not completely disloyal to Fray Marcos or to his commission to open the way and pacify the Indians so that the friar might travel in safety. Fray Marcos himself made this clear with the statement that as he traveled on in hot pursuit of his ambassador he always found "good lodging, excellent reception, and many turquoises, hides of the cattle and the same information regarding the country."

Everywhere Fray Marcos found the Indians fully informed of his mission and waiting to welcome him with festivities and feasting, to honor him as a guest. Estevanico performed his duties as an advance man with efficiency and thoroughness.

There, however, his compliance with instructions ended. He would not let Fray Marcos catch him.

Profoundly exasperated, Fray Marcos pushed on into the *despoblado*, on across the Rio Mayo, along the Rio Cedros trail, across the Rio Yaqui, day after day being warmly received, well fed and comfortably lodged, day after day continuing to see turquoises and buffalo robes, and hearing more of the Seven Cities, and day after day finding that Estevanico was keeping well ahead of him.

At last came another message: Estevanico would wait for him in Pueblo de los Corazones.

After a hard journey of four days through another arid area, Fray Marcos and his escort came down into the valley of the Rio Sonora and arrived at Corazones.

The unmitigated Moor scoundrel had vanished.

Estevanico had been there, no doubt of that. Fray Marcos received a rousing welcome. He settled down to a badly needed rest. Apparently Estevanico had not dallied long among his old friends, the Opatas, but had raised a bit of merry hell and marched on.

Now Estevanico was traversing country never before entered by a European, white or black, a country completely unknown to any people except the few Indians who lived in it or passed through it on trading missions.

Estevanico was going into a land that was a blank space on the maps of the world.

XIII

Fray Marcos admired the Valle de Sonora and the people living in it no less than had Cabeza de Vaca.

"It is so thickly settled with intelligent people," he said, "and so well supplied with provisions that it could furnish food for more than three hundred horsemen."

How prophetic were his words! Not many months would pass before the army of Coronado would arrive there, and Pueblo de los Corazones would become its supply base and main field headquarters.

If he was sorely vexed by Estevanico's inexcusable behavior, Fray Marcos was not disappointed with what he learned from the people of Corazones. "They knew as much about Cibola as they know in New Spain about Mexico, or in Peru about Cuzco," he wrote.

The friendly Opatas in the Valle de Sonora described

for him "in much detail the construction of Cibola's houses and the town's streets and plazas like people who had been there many times and had brought from there fine things they obtained in exchange for personal service."

For some unexplained reason, Fray Marcos had begun to have some doubts, and he expressed the opinion that "it was not possible for the houses to be constructed the way they had been described" to him. Thereupon, his Corazones hosts "took dirt and ashes, mixed with water, and showed me how they set the stone and reared the building."

Still suspicious, Fray Marcos asked if the people of Cibola "had wings to ascend to those terraces." The Opatas laughed "and pictured a ladder for me as clearly as I might do it myself."

Fray Marcos also was told "of the woolen cloth of Totonteac, where, they said, the houses were like those of Cibola, but better, and that there were many more of them, and that it was a very extensive place, without limit." He was hearing about the Hopi villages. The wool for the cloth grew on the backs of animals the size of Estevanico's greyhounds.

Now a strange animal came into the talks. If it was not a product of Fray Marcos's imagination, it was part of some legend with which the inhabitants of the Valle de Sonora sought to entertain their distinguished guest.

"They brought me a hide," declared the friar, "half as large again as that of a big cow. They told me it came from an animal which has only one horn in the front, and that this horn is curved towards its breast, then turns in a straight point. They say it is so strong that it tears anything it strikes, however strong it may be. They say that there are many of these animals in that country. In color the skin rather resembles that of a buck, and the hair is as long as the finger is thick."

If it could be definitely established that Fray Marcos suffered from nightmares or hallucinations, he could be excused for such flights of fancy, even though he recorded them as factual. However, the following statements on the geography of the country remain as evidence to show that he was not afflicted with a disordered nervous system, was not a victim of paranoic delusions. He was a plain liar. And more proof of this sickness was to come from his own pen.

While in the Valle de Sonora, he said, he had learned "that the coast turns west very abruptly, for up to the time of entering the first *despoblado,* the coast extended always to the north. Since the turning of the coast is very important, I wanted to verify it, *and so I went in search of it, and I saw clearly that at a latitude of thirty-five degrees it turns to the west.* This brought me no less joy than the good information of the country."

Fray Marcos was in the Valle de Sonora only five days. Yet, he claimed that in that time he made a side journey of at least four hundred miles.

Strangely, he furnished no other details of this remarkable trip, gave no description of the country through which he passed on it, nor, and most important, he made no mention of the Indians he met.

From Pueblo de los Corazones to the nearest point on the coast was a distance which took natives four days to travel. The land does not make a major swing to the west in this area. In fact, no westward coastal swing of significance occurs for a great distance to the north.

Fray Marcos could not have made such a journey, or even a small part of it, without being seen by the Seri Indians who inhabited the coast and the off-shore islands. A year later, Seris visited the camp of Coronado's advance company. If they had heard of Fray Marcos, they had never seen him. No white man had ever passed through their country on land.

If Fray Marcos had gone to where the coast turns sharply west, he would have reached the present Puerto Penasco, very near the head of the Gulf of California.

If he had reached thirty-five degrees, as he said he did, he would have been far north of the head of the Gulf, almost to Flagstaff, Arizona.

He didn't go to the coast. He never saw it.

As he went on in pursuit of the maddening Estevanico, Fray Marcos learned that above the Valle de Sonora lay a forbidding desert land, a vast *despoblado* very difficult to pass through. The news did nothing to decrease his aggravation.

Near the beginning of the gruelling journey he received more messengers from Estevanico. They informed him that the Moor was already crossing the great waste region, and that Estevanico was "very elated, because he was more certain of the riches of the country than before."

According to Fray Marcos, Estevanico sent word that "since he had taken leave of me he had never caught the Indians in a lie, that thus far he had found everything as it had been described to him, and that he expected to find the rest the same. I believe it to be true, because the fact is that from the very first day when I heard of

Cibola, until now, everything that the Indians told me I have verified. I have traveled one hundred twelve leagues, which makes the veracity of these people quite worth recording."

That was praise Fray Marcos could not have given to himself. A hundred and twelve leagues obviously did not include the hundreds of miles he traveled in a side trip from Corazones to find that the coast turned sharply west just south of Flagstaff, where the only water to be found is in small streams in deep canyons.

The couriers who brought word that Estevanico was far into the great *despoblado* also reported that more than three hundred Indians were traveling with the Negro. Three hundred! And heaven knew how many concubines!

Fray Marcos's anger soared to new heights. If it had not occurred to him before, it was now clear to him what Estevanico intended to do.

The unconscionable black heathen had never planned to wait for him, had never meant to keep his promises. He had always intended to go on alone . . . rather, with a parade of more than three hundred warriors and wenches . . . and be first to reach Cibola. No telling what riches the Moor disbeliever would confiscate. He might well set himself up as king of the new land, win fame and glory, not to mention the favor of Mendoza. It was all very disheartening and unfair.

The trail which Estevanico took and over which the fuming Fray Marcos pursued him, after leaving the pass above Pueblo de los Corazones, ran northward out of the Valle de Sonora in the vicinity of the present villages [some of which existed then] of Baviscora, Aconchi,

Huepac, Banamichi, Sinoquippe, Arizpe, Bacoachic, and the mining town of Cananea.

Once the Mexican mountains were passed the *despoblado* began. It continued, the Indians told Fray Marcos, all the way to Cibola, and was far more perilous than any he had passed through to the south. Very few people lived in it, for its resources of water, game and fuel were too poor to support more than a small population.

The residents of the Valle de Sonora had graciously agreed to furnish him with the necessary supplies for the difficult trek, as well as men to carry them. Some thirty headmen had elected to make the trip with him, and they had adorned themselves in their finest raiment, and wore long strings of turquoises.

Both his fears and his irritation steadily increasing, Fray Marcos pressed forward into the forbidding land with all possible speed, "because," as he later admitted, "each day seemed to me a year."

XIV

On a May day in the year 1539, Estevanico the Black unlocked for the world the gateway to the Southwest of the future United States.

From a great ridge in the Huachuca Mountains, where the air is thin and sweet with the perfumes of evergreens and flowers, the place where he crossed the present international border may be seen in a magnificent panoramic view.

A part of this high country overlooking Sonora and southern Arizona has been set aside as a perpetual memorial. But not to him. The area is called Coronado National Monument.

Coronado did not pass that way until more than a year after Estevanico had traversed the trail.

Moreover, Coronado's expedition was not the second

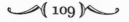

to follow the old Indian trading route to Cibola. It was the fourth. After Estevanico came Fray Marcos. In the winter of 1539-1540, Melchior Diaz with fifteen mounted Spanish soldiers and perhaps twice that number of Indians rode as far north as the ancient ruin of Chichilticale, at Eagle Pass, the opening between the Santa Teresa and Pinaleno Mountains.*

Estevanico the Black led the way. After crossing the divide which separates Sonora and Arizona, the trail he took went down the San Pedro River. The names of the present communities along the way are Hereford, Charleston, Fairbank and St. David. In the vicinity of Benson, his guides led him to the northeast, across Arivaipa Valley, to Eagle Pass. From Chichilticale [Red House] the trail swung northward to the Gila River and went on across the high plateau country to the Little Colorado, near St. Johns. Turning northeasterly again, it crossed Carrizo Creek and reached the Zuni River, which came out of Cibola.

It requires no great imagination to envision the dramatic colorful pageant crawling through the fearsome *despoblado,* across the angular tilted mesas, up the hot valleys, over ridge and sweeping plain, through the canyons. Surrounded by more than three hundred red people marched the intrepid and fearless black, his greyhounds panting at his side, his plumes answering the moving desert airs, the strings of turquoise and coral over his chest, bells tinkling on his ankles, sweat gleaming on his powerful dark limbs. With each stride he wrote history in the dust.

Up the Zuni River . . . and then on a rise beyond a

*Northeast of the present town of Benson, Arizona.

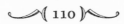

vast undulating sweep his eyes found the walls of the first city of Cibola. It was called Hawikuh.

Remnants of those walls may be seen today. They lie scattered and broken some twelve miles southwest of the town of Zuni. A visitor may stand among the rubble and gaze upon the ground where the trail of Estevanico the Black came to an end.

It cannot be authentically stated where Fray Marcos was when Estevanico reached Hawikuh. The friar's own claims may not be believed. There is evidence which goes far in disproving them.

His report indicated that he traveled some fourteen or fifteen days across the *despoblado* ... incidentally, "always well supplied with food — deer, hares, and partridges ..." which his Indian companions thoughtfully had brought along for him. He mentions that the Cibola Trail was well marked "with old houses and many vestiges of fire, left by the people who went by this road ..." Undoubtedly these were campsites used by trading parties.

A journey of fifteen days would have taken him to within three days of Hawikuh.

He did not get that far north. If he did, then all the chroniclers who followed him were consistent in perpetrating the same falsehoods. Their writings indicate that he did not travel farther north than the Gila River, probably not within a hundred and fifty miles of Hawikuh.

Wherever they were that fateful day, Fray Marcos and his retinue, they suddenly saw approaching an Indian runner.

The courier brought the news that Estevanico had been killed in Hawikuh.

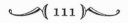

Fray Marcos maintained that it was with difficulty he calmed the people with him enough to hear an account of the tragedy.

According to Fray Marcos, the courier said: " . . . one day's travel before reaching Cibola, Esteban sent messengers ahead with his gourd, just as he was in the habit of doing, so that they might know he was coming. The gourd had some strings of jingle bells, and two feathers, one white and the other red."

The messengers were to inform the people of Cibola that Estevanico wished only peace, and that he was a great medicine man who could perform magical cures.

When the "Lord of Cibola" had received the gourd, instead of being overjoyed he became violently angry. Fray Marcos reported:

"When he took it in his hands and saw the jingle bells, he at once hurled the gourd to the ground with much wrath. He told the messengers to leave immediately, for he knew what sort of people they represented, and that they should tell them not to enter the city or he would kill them all."

Fray Marcos did not trouble to append to this statement the explanation it requires. If it is possible the Zuni Indians had heard of white men, they certainly had never seen one. It is even more certain they had never seen a black man. Word that white and black men existed might have reached them in two ways over trading routes. The appearance of the four men among the pueblos of the Jumanos on the Rio Grande might have been known to them. Similar news might have come over the same trail followed by Estevanico from the Opatas or other Indians in the Valle de Sonora. Indeed, it seems logical to believe they did know that humans of a strange breed, or breeds, had come out of the East, for such exciting intelligence would not have been kept a secret by commercial travelers or hunters who knew it.

These possibilities may not be excluded, but the gourd itself would not have told the Zunis "what sort of people" the intruders, either white or black, were, nor would it have told them anything of their intentions. The decorations and colors on the gourd might have identified its origin and the people who fashioned it, however, and these might have been people the Zunis did not wish to see in their land.

The messengers who had taken the gourd to Cibola went back to Estevanico and told him what had happened. He had laughed. The same thing had happened more than once when he had been with Cabeza de Vaca, and on each occasion Indians who had been suspicious or unfriendly at first always had been humble and hospitable in the end.

Estevanico, said Fray Marcos, told his caravan that "it was of no importance, that those who showed anger received him better.

"So Esteban continued on his journey until he came to the city of Cibola."

Estevanico was puzzled by the reception he received. Not only had the gourd's magic failed, but the Zunis were not impressed by him.

". . . the people refused to allow him to enter the city," Fray Marcos said the courier informed him, "and put him in a large house outside of it, taking away from him everything he carried to trade, turquoises and other things he had obtained from Indians along the way.

They kept him there that night without giving him, or those who came with him, any food or water."

It is very unlikely that Estevanico thought of trading turquoises. The traffic in this valuable article moved in the opposite direction. The Indians traveling with him had considerable food with them, and the river was nearby.

Fray Marcos continued: "The next morning this Indian [presumably the courier who brought the bad news] was thirsty and left the house to get a drink from a nearby river. From that place he shortly afterward saw Esteban fleeing and people from the city pursuing him, and they killed some of those who came with him. Upon seeing this, this Indian, concealing himself, fled up the river and then crossed over it, reaching the road of the *despoblado*."

If he fled up the river he would have been going away from the *despoblado* trail. Possibly he went upstream for a distance, then crossed and went downstream. However, if he remained along the river it is remarkable that he was not observed and taken prisoner. In such a time of excitement, the Zunis would have been exceptionally alert, and would have kept in mind the possibility that other invaders were close on Estevanico's heels.

In recounting the tragedy, Fray Marcos did not overlook a rare opportunity to describe his own courage: "On hearing this news, some of the Indians who were with me began to weep. In view of this wretched news I thought I should be lost. I feared not so much to lose my life, as not to be able to return and report on the greatness of the country, where God our Lord can be so well served, His Holy faith exalted and the royal patrimony of His Majesty increased.

"I distributed among the chiefs [with me] all the clothing and articles of trade I carried, and told them not to be afraid but to accompany me, which they did."

If Fray Marcos was hoping that the "wretched news" brought by the courier would turn out to be erroneous, that Estevanico, upon whom he depended so greatly for the success of the mission, might be found alive, he was soon disappointed.

After traveling on toward Cibola with his frightened escort, he came upon two more Indians who had been with Estevanico. Bloodstained and suffering from wounds, they "confirmed the unhappy news that Esteban, and all those who were with him, who numbered more than three hundred men, besides many women, had been killed by those of Cibola, and only they had escaped."

This was a terrible situation indeed ... only three survivors out of more than three hundred! It would have been a major catastrophe, if it had been true.

In the face of such great peril, Fray Marcos, according to his own story, still refused to turn back. He said: "I finally persuaded two of the chiefs to accompany me, and with my own Indians and interpreters, I proceeded on my journey until coming within view of Cibola, which is situated on a plain, at the base of a round hill."

Just the reverse was the case: Hawikuh stood on a round hill overlooking a plain.

Now in Fray Marcos's report, come the passages which set New Spain on fire: "This pueblo has a fine appearance, the best I have seen in these regions. The houses are as they have been described to me by the Indians, all of stone, with terraces and flat roofs, as it seemed to me from a hill where I stood to view it.

"The city is larger than the city of Mexico."

Fray Marcos assertedly found himself faced with a difficult decision. "At times," he said, "I was tempted to go to the pueblo, because I knew I was risking only my life, and this I had offered to God the day I began the journey. In the end, realizing my danger, I feared that if I died no information would be obtained regarding this land which in my opinion is the greatest and best of all that have been discovered."

This was unadulterated nonsense. He had been in the West Indies, in Peru and through Mexico and Guatemala, and he well knew the size of the fortunes taken from them. He was comparing a single pueblo . . . and not a very large one, either . . . in the arid southwestern country with the immense natural resources, the mines and the cities, of the tropical and mountainous countries to the south.

Fray Marcos bolstered his assertions with this statement: "When I told the chieftains who were with me how well impressed I was with Cibola, they told me that it was the smallest of the Seven Cities, and that Totonteac is much larger and better than all the seven, that it has so many houses and people that there is no end to it."

Despite his fears and his decision to go no farther, Fray Marcos allegedly did not fail to carry out his orders. He wrote what he knew Mendoza would most like to hear:

"I thought it appropriate to name that land the new Kingdom of St. Francis. And so, with the aid of the

Indians, I gathered there a pile of stones, and on top of it I erected a small and slender cross, as I had no materials with which to make a larger one.* I declared that I was erecting that cross and landmark as a sign of possession, in the name of Don Antonio de Mendoza, viceroy and governor of New Spain, for the emperor, our Lord . . . I stated that I was taking possession there of all the Seven Cities and of the Kingdoms of Totonteac, Acus, and Marata, but I was not going to visit them, in order that I might return to give a report of what had been done and seen."

After assertedly gazing on the magnificence of Hawikuh, and taking possession of the country, Fray Marcos had turned about and had fled, "with more fear than food," back towards Mexico. His reception this time among the people of the Valle de Sonora was, according to him, quite unpleasant. The reason was that "both men and women were weeping bitterly for their people who had been killed at Cibola." He maintained that they held him responsible for the catastrophe . . . Estevanico was not there to be blamed . . . and threats were made against his life.

Fray Marcos claimed that he got out of this perilous situation by making some threats of his own. Assertedly he warned the Opatas that if they killed him he would go to Heaven, and then other Spaniards would come looking for him, and "would kill them all."

"Being afraid," he continued, "I quickly took leave of the people of that valley."

*It may be an insignificant point, but cottonwoods and other large arid land trees grew along rivers of the area and where there was seepage water.

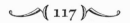

He traveled south as fast as his sandaled feet would carry him, averaging eight to ten leagues a day.

Fray Marcos had not forgotten that when he had reached the Rio Fuerte on the outward journey Indians had told him "that four or five days inland, where the cordilleras of the sierras end, there is an open valley [abra] in which they said there were many large settlements with people clothed in cotton." These people, the Indians had said, had vessels made of gold, and wore round articles of gold hanging from their noses and ears.

The *abra* was on the Rio Mayo, and he would have liked to take the time to visit it, but he had passed it up because of his eagerness to complete the main purpose of the mission, which was to discover the Seven Cities. As he came to the Rio Mayo on his return journey, anxious as he was to get back to Compostela, he, nevertheless, decided to take the time to check on the report of the rich people who dwelt in the *abra*.

This, of course, was not the truth, but a part of a desperate scheme he had conceived. The fact was that he had discovered nothing of value in the north, and he was hoping that he might uncover something worthwhile in the *abra*, anything that would provide a bit of substance for his wild claims.

"I did not dare to enter it [the *abra*]," he said, "for fear of endangering my person and failing to report what I had seen [at Cibola], since it seemed to me that Spaniards would first have to settle and rule this other land of the Seven Cities, and that this valley [Rio Mayo] could be better explored.

"So I saw only from the mouth of the *abra*, seven fair-sized settlements, and somewhat distant a valley below, very fresh and of very good land, whence came many smokes. I was told that there is much gold there ... I erected two crosses and took possession of all this *abra* and valley."

Even where there was nothing more than a few scraggly Indian villages, Fray Marcos saw "seven fair-sized settlements." The numeral apparently obsessed him.

In Culiacan, the fully recovered Fray Onorato rejoined him, and together they hurried on to Compostela. It was near the end of June, 1539, when they reached the provincial capital and reported to Coronado. Fray Marcos wrote immediately of his arrival "to the Most Illustrious Señor Viceroy of New Spain, and to our Father Fray Antonio de Ciudad-Rodrigo, provincial, asking them to send orders" telling him what to do next.

The Viceroy, the Father Provincial and Governor Coronado soon told him.

Coronado had returned to Compostela from a brief exploring trip shortly after the two friars reached there. Castaneda recorded what happened:

"Governor Coronado found the friars who had just arrived, and who told such great things about what the negro Estevan had discovered and what they had heard from the Indians, and other things they had heard about the South Sea and islands and other riches, that, without stopping for anything, the governor set off at once for the City of Mexico, taking Friar Marcos with him, to tell the viceroy about it."

Noteworthy in this statement is the absence of any claim as to what he, Marcos, himself had discovered. It refers only to what Estevanico had discovered and what Marcos had *heard* from Indians.

Castaneda continued: "He [Coronado] made the things seem more important by not talking about them to anyone except his particular friends, under promise of the greatest secrecy, until after he had reached Mexico and seen Don Antonio de Mendoza. Then it began to be noised abroad that the Seven Cities . . . had already been discovered."

Whether he suspected Fray Marcos of lying or not, Coronado was not taking any chances. He wanted the Viceroy to hear Fray Marcos's story first hand.

XV

.THE WORD was out: the Seven Cities had been found. Mexico City, from the viceroy's palace to the lowest slave quarters, was wild with excitement. Conquest fever raged with the result, said Castaneda, "that more than 300 Spaniards and about 800 natives of New Spain collected in a few days. There were so many men of high quality among the Spaniards, that such a noble body was never collected in the Indies, nor so many men of quality in such a small body . . . Coronado was captain-general, because he had been the author of it all . . ."

The great Coronado Expedition was born, and as the members moved toward a rendezvous in Compostela, from which the actual start to the north would be made, Fray Marcos was in command of the little band of friars who would go with it.

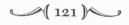

Still the Viceroy Mendoza could not overcome entirely his deep feeling that cautiousness was required. It may have been, recognizing the imaginative powers of Fray Marcos and knowing the friar's talent for dramatizing commonplace incidents, that he secretly suspected him of fabricating fine tales.

Although the expedition was being readied, and he had no intention of changing his mind about it, Mendoza ordered that the veteran frontiersman, Melchior Diaz, take a small company of horsemen and check on the reports of Fray Marcos. Captain Diaz was alcalde mayor of Culiacan. As Mendoza well knew, he was a man of integrity, a realist and he would not be taken in by wild stories. If the truth was obtainable, Diaz would get it, and would report accurately what he found, and nothing else.

Diaz did.

It was mid-November of 1539, a poor time of the year to be starting north, when Diaz, his mounted soldiers and Indians, perhaps forty-five in all, left Culiacan.

This is an important chapter in the history of American exploration, important not because of Diaz's discoveries, not because of his daring venture, but important because he and his men rode the first horses to trod the soil of the land that would become the western United States.

Mendoza's order directed Diaz to see if the accounts given by Fray Marcos "agreed with what he might discover." With the stroke of his pen, the Viceroy sent a small reconnaissance party on a simple mission that would turn out to be a major event in the annals of his time. One cannot help wondering if he was aware of its significance. Well might one wonder, too, if Diaz held such thoughts as he rode northward.

Diaz and his company traveled fast. If the Indians of northern Sonora had heard of horses . . . and they probably had heard of them from people living farther to the south who had encountered Spanish slave hunters . . . they had never seen one.

Now they heard a strange kind of thunder on the old trail along the Rio Sonora, a rhythmic beating on the earth in tempos they had never known. Now there were nights in the valleys of Sonora when the lights of campfires caught on the sleek sides of the great beasts tethered about the mat houses, and there were new sounds in the shadows, the sounds of fodder being munched, the sounds of stamping, and there were the strange smells of an unknown kind of sweat and an unknown kind of manure.

In a comparatively few days the snorting, prancing monsters had borne their riders over a distance that would have required weeks to traverse on foot. Always before, Indians who had met Spaniards had reckoned their power in terms of the gun, but that measure was no longer adequate nor accurate.

The horse gave the Spaniard power and mobility which, when combined with the deadliness and effectiveness of the musket, made him invincible. If anything was incontrovertible proof of the ingenuity and creative powers of the white man's God, it was the horse.

And in the beginning, when it first came, and even for some years thereafter, the horse was a sacred symbol to the Indians. Before he had acquired them for himself, and had reshaped his own way of life to utilize them to good advantage, the western Indian held the horse in reverent awe.

It had not been a good harvest year in the Sonora Valley, but in Pueblo de los Carazones Diaz was able to obtain some supplies, reporting that the people, although lacking their normal bountiful stores of foodstuffs, shared with him "fodder and an abundance of maize wherever they had any."

Diaz pressed on from Sonora into the feared *despoblado*, on into Arizona.

He did not reach Hawikuh. Winter defeated him. As he went northward the weather grew steadily colder. Several of his men died from exposure. At the ancient ruin of Chichilticale, in southeastern Arizona, his journey was completely halted by snow and low temperatures.

Indians he met there and along the way told him that cotton grew in Cibola. In the same breath, they told him that the land of the Seven Cities was cold country. This was conflicting testimony he determined to solve, and he did. However, in this instance, as he shivered in a flimsy mat shelter with a blizzard howling across the vast barrens, he might have been excused if he had believed cotton could not grow in such a cruel country.

Diaz was an indefatigable reporter, refusing to let the adverse circumstances of his assignment prevent him from gathering every shred of information available. He spent several miserable weeks at Chichilticale, and then turned back, but not empty-handed.

At every opportunity he had questioned Indians, giving special attention to those who said they had been to Cibola. Some, he wrote Mendoza, had told him they had been going to Hawikuh "fifteen and twenty years."

He secured his intelligence "in many different ways, taking some Indians together and others separately..." When he compared their statements, "they all seem to agree in what they say."

Some of Diaz's informants were Piman Indians who had gone to Hawikuh with Estevanico.

Father Marcos had stated that he made careful inquiry among the Indians. It seems relevant to note here that he would have had opportunities to question many of the same Indians to whom Diaz talked. The padre could have learned a great deal about Cibola from persons who had been traveling to the kingdom "fifteen or twenty years" on trading missions.

Diaz demonstrated that one need not have seen Hawikuh to obtain good descriptions of it and to have gathered a large amount of information about the Kingdom of Cibola without visiting it.

As far as Diaz was able to learn, the death of Estevanico had occurred much in the manner of Fray Marcos's account. As for the story that more than three hundred Indians had died with Estevanico at Hawikuh, Diaz said nothing in his report to the Viceroy. He probably had a good reason for omitting it: respect for the word of a man of the church. Better to remain silent than to call a father a liar. There can be no doubt that in his interrogations Diaz learned that the slaughter had not taken place.

Diaz reported that after Estevanico's death, the people of Cibola had sent word to other Indians to the south "that if any Christians should come, they ought not to consider them as anything peculiar, and ought to kill them, because they were mortal..."

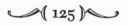

Christians, black or white, were not gods, not children of the sun, not powerful shamans. They were made of flesh and blood, as all other men. Incontrovertible proof of this was in the Cibolans' hands, "because they kept the bones of the one who had come there."

If Indians who encountered Christians feared to kill them "they should send word so that those at Cibola could come and do it."

"I can very easily believe that all this has taken place," Diaz told Mendoza, "and that there has been some communication between these places, because of the coolness with which they received us and the sour faces they have shown us."

No one attempted to kill Diaz and his men, however. Perhaps the presence of horses had a bearing on the situation. The appearance of the miraculous beasts greatly influenced the thinking of the Indians, and stirred in them fears they had never experienced.

Diaz gathered some artifacts which Indians said had come from Cibola . . . some turquoises, crystals, a wig or two and a few pieces of raiment. But he could learn nothing of such desirable things as emeralds, gold and silver. Indeed, not a single native had even intimated to him that the people of Cibola possessed precious metals and jewels of any kind. Moreover, he saw fewer strings of turquoise than Fray Marcos had reported were worn by the Indians.

Hawikuh, Fray Marcos had said, was "larger than the city of Mexico." This absurd statement could have meant only one of two things. Either he had not seen it, even from a distant hilltop, or he was speaking a falsehood.

And the statement of Fray Marcos made all the more apparent the objectives of Diaz's report to Mendoza.

"... there are seven places," Diaz told the Viceroy, "being a short day's march from one to another, all of which are together called Cibola. The houses are of stone and mud, coarsely worked. They are made in this way: One large wall, and at each end of this wall some rooms are built, partioned off twenty feet square, according to the descriptions they [his Indian informants] give, which are planked with square beams. Most of the houses are reached from flat roofs, using their ladders to go to the streets. The houses have three and four stories. They declare that there are a few having two stories. The stories are mostly half as high again as a man, except the first one, which is low, and only a little more than a man's height. One ladder is used to communicate with ten or twelve houses together. They make use of the lowest one and live in the highest ones. In the lowest ones of all they have some loopholes made sideways, as in the fortresses of Spain. The Indians say that when these people are attacked, they station themselves in their houses and fight from there."

The people of Hawikuh, said Diaz, had salt available to them, but water was not plentiful.* They did not raise cotton, but obtained it from Totonteac [Hopi Pueblos]. The Cibolans did not "know what sea fish is."†

*The Zunis had adequate water. Diaz was talking with Indians from the Gila drainage basin who were used to strong streams flowing from high country where the snowfall was heavy. To them the streams of Cibola would have seemed small.

†This was erroneous information, for many kinds of sea shells, fish bones, fish skins, fish meal, coral and other marine products reached the Pueblos over ancient trading trails from both the Pacific coast and the Gulf of California. Probably Diaz's informants meant that the Cibolans did not have sea fish to eat.

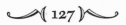

Diaz learned that although buffalo skins and robes were to be found in Cibola, the bison "were beyond the province." Products from the buffalo plains east of the mountains reached the Pueblos through trading channels.*

On his return trip, Diaz met the army of Coronado advancing northward on the coastal road at Chiametla. The report he made to the Governor-General was truthful and uninspiring. It did nothing to bolster the spirits that were already sagging because of the hardships of the march.

Some effort was made to keep Coronado's soldiers from hearing the discouraging information Diaz brought back, but it was not successful.

Castaneda, who was there, recounted that Diaz, his lieutenant, Juan de Saldivar, and the troopers "went as far as Chichilticale, which is where the wilderness begins, and there they turned back, not finding anything important. They reached Chiametla just as the army was ready to leave, and reported to the general. Although it was kept a secret, the bad news leaked out, and there were some reports [obviously circulated by soldiers] which, although they were exaggerated, did not fail to give an indication of what the facts were."

Fray Marcos was there in Chiametla, too, and this was a situation he was not willing to endure in silence. Reflections were being cast on his good name and his veracity.

"Friar Marcos," said Castaneda, "noticing that some were feeling disturbed, cleared away these clouds, promising that what they would see should be good, and that

*See the author's *Traders of the Western Morning.*

he would place the army in a country where their hands would be filled, and in this way he quieted them so that they appeared well satisfied."

Whatever his afflictions and inadequacies, Fray Marcos was not lacking in brass.

Coronado was intrigued by the report Fray Marcos had made of gold and large settlements in the *abra* of the Rio Mayo valley. Although both he and Mendoza had suspected that Fray Marcos had been misinformed or had exaggerated, Coronado decided that the matter was worth investigating. Again the competent and trustworthy Melchior Diaz was selected to conduct an exploration.

At the Rio Fuertes, Diaz was ordered to take ten horsemen and make a swift reconnaissance of the *abra*, several days' ride inland. Fray Marcos did not go on this trip, for he was dedicated to traveling on foot, as he believed any worthy apostle of the Lord should do. This was accepted as a worthy excuse, but there were probably other reasons why he did not care to go.

Adhering to Fray Marcos's directions, Diaz and his scouts rode hard for four days through high mountains. They found no rich lush valley containing large settlements. Nor did they find, as Coronado wrote, "anything to live on, or any people, or any information about anything except two or three poor villages with twenty or thirty huts each. From the natives he [Diaz] learned there was nothing to be found in the country beyond except the mountains, which continued to be very rough and entirely uninhabited, and . . . this labor was lost . . ."

The soldiers and gentlemen of the Coronado Expedition were more than ever disgruntled and discouraged by Diaz's report about the *abra*. Coronado stated plainly that the "whole company felt disturbed, that a thing so much praised, and about which Fray Marcos had said so much, should be found so very different; and they began to think that all the rest would be of the same sort."

If only they could have looked a bit into the future!

As the expedition continued its difficult march north from the Rio Fuertes, the members wondered what had happened to the good roads which Fray Marcos had said they would find on the way to Cibola. Coronado wrote to Mendoza that he and his men were finding the way very hard, "impossible to travel without making a new road or repairing the one already there. This troubles the soldiers not a little because everything which the friar had said was found to be quite the reverse; for among other things he had said and declared was that the way would be plain and good, *and there would be only one small hill of about half a league.*" In the Sierra Madre! "But the truth is that there are mountains which, however well the trail might be repaired, could not be crossed without great danger that the horses would fall over the cliffs. Indeed, it was so bad that many of the animals which your Lordship sent as food for the army were lost on this part of the route, because of the roughness of the rocks. The lambs and wethers lost their hoofs along the way, and most of those I had brought from Culiacan I left at the river of Lachimi [Yaquimi] because they were unable to travel*

*The distinguished historian, Bolton, suggests that Fray Marcos would have made a great movie actor. I don't agree. Movie actors are paid to pretend. If we must place Fray Marcos in some Twentieth Century job, I suggest that he would have been eminently successful as an advertising copywriter for the *All Year Club of Southern California.*

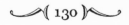

Not only badly needed meat animals died because of the roughness of the country and the trail, which Fray Marcos had said would be good, but a number of valuable horses were lost, and, as Coronado sadly recorded: "Some of our Negroes and some of the Indians also died here, which was no small loss . . ."

The popularity of Fray Marcos was steadily disintegrating, but it had a long way to fall yet.

In considering the time when Coronado was within a few days' march of Hawikuh, the first pueblo of Cibola, an odd situation presents itself. This was the area in which Fray Marcos was supposed to have received the initial message that Estevanico had been slain.

But the Coronado Expedition chronicles of this part of the march do not mention the event.

When Coronado was within three days' journey of Hawikuh, at the place where Fray Marcos said he had met the two wounded Indians who had been with Estevanico, the journals make no reference whatever to the sad meeting.

Moreover, Fray Marcos is not even mentioned by name in the accounts of the trip along this part of the road to Cibola. This is made all the more strange by the fact that Fray Marcos was with the Coronado expedition.

The anger of the soldiers and gentlemen caused by Fray Marcos's deceptions were hardly more than a mild wind compared to the cyclone of fury stirred in them by their first sight of the grubby pueblo of Hawikuh.

Where was the great city which Fray Marcos had said was larger than Mexico City?

Castaneda tells how the weary, bruised and hungry men felt as they gazed in bitter disappointment on

Hawikuh: ". . . such were the curses that some hurled at Friar Marcos that I pray God may protect him from them.

"It is a little, crowded village, looking as if it had been crumpled all up together. There are haciendas in New Spain that make a better appearance at a distance."

XVI

IN JULY, 1540, Coronado fought the residents of Hawikuh and captured the pueblo ... a good year after Estevanico had died there. On August 3, he wrote to the
Viceroy Mendoza a report of the conquest. It was the
best contemporary description of the city ... which
Coronado, always the diplomat and politician, even
under the burden of a crushing disappointment ...
christened Granada, in honor of Mendoza's home town.

"It now remains," he wrote the Viceroy, "for me to
tell about this city and kingdom and province, of which
the Father Provincial [Fray Marcos] gave Your Lordship an account.

"In brief, I can assure you that in reality he has not
told the truth in a single thing that he said, but everything is the reverse of what he said, except the name of

the city and the large stone houses. For, although they are not decorated with turquoises, nor made of lime nor of good bricks, nevertheless they are very good houses, with three and four and five stories, where there are very good apartments and good rooms with corridors, and some very good rooms under ground and paved, which are made for winter, something like a sort of hot baths.*

"The ladders which they have for their houses are all movable and portable, which are taken up and placed wherever they please. They are made of two pieces of of wood, with rounds like ours.

"The Seven Cities are seven little villages, all having the kind of houses I have described . . . This one which I have called a city I have named Granada because it has some similarity to it, as well as out of regard for Your Lordship."†

In Hawikuh, Coronado told Mendoza, there were "perhaps two hundred houses, all surrounded by a wall, and it seems to me that with the other houses, which are not so surrounded, there might be altogether five hundred families. There is another town nearby, which is one of the seven, but somewhat larger than this, and another of the same size as this, but the other four are somewhat smaller . . .

"The people of the towns seem to me to be of ordinary size and intelligent . . .

"They do not raise cotton . . ."

*Here Coronado is speaking of kivas, underground ceremonial and council chambers, still to be found in the pueblos inhabited today.

†One of Coronado's "trusted companions," whom Hodge (biblio.) suggests was Garcia Lopez de Cardenas, wrote that Hawikuh was named Granada not only out of regard for the Viceroy, but because it "resembles the Albaicin," which is a part of Granada near the Alhambra.

Coronado thought the climate of Zuni was much like that of the Valley of Mexico. There were "no kinds of fruit or fruit trees. The country is all level, and is nowhere shut in by high mountains, although there are some hills and rough passages. There are not many birds ... There are no trees fit for firewood here, because they can bring enough for their needs from a clump of very small cedars four leagues distant. Very good grass is found a quarter of a league away, where there is pasturage for our horses as well as mowing for hay ... They have very good salt in crystals, which they bring from a lake a day's journey distant from here ... They have many animals — bears, tigers, lions, porcupines, and some sheep as big as a horse, with very large horns and little tails."

The Zunis are a people of heterogeneous blood. The distinguished ethnologist, Frank H. Cushing (biblio.) wrote that they were descended from two parental stocks, one of which came from the north and the other from the lower Colorado River region. But there were numerous accretions from other tribes and stocks, in both historic and pre-historic times. Reports of the Bureau of American Ethnology describe the Zuni as "quiet, good tempered, and industrious." They are a distinct linguistic family. They adhere tenaciously to their ancient religion, which is closely interwoven with their social organization. Estevanico learned of this phase of their character in a tragic way. The sacred medicine gourd, which he carried and which so angered them, was one of the causes of his murder.

News of Estevanico's death traveled swiftly through the southwest desert country.

In command of three supply ships, Hernando de Alarcon was sailing along the east coast of the Gulf of California, hoping to give support to Coronado. In August, 1540, he reached the head of the gulf. Coronado was then at Hawikuh. Impassable shoals confronted Alarcon, and leaving the vessels he had gone on in small boats, up the Rio Colorado . . . which he called Buena Guia (Unfailing Guide) . . . praying that it would lead him into the Province of Cibola and a union with Coronado.

He ascended the Colorado as far as the mouth of the Gila, being the first explorer to reach the Yuman tribes. The discovery of the Colorado by Alarcon, and his entrance into country that would become part of the State of California, in contrast to most Spanish conquests, was accomplished without undue violence and bloodshed. There were some perilous moments, but he was able to convince the Indians that he had no wish to fight and that he came as a friend.

In his councils with the peoples along the Colorado in September, Alarcon met three men who said they had been to Cibola. The Gila was a part of one of the oldest trading routes from the Pacific coast to the tribes of central Arizona and the land of the Pueblos.

One of Alarcon's informants told him that a chief in Cibola had a greyhound and several green dinner plates. Estevanico's!

Another of the men who had journeyed to Cibola told him of a black man who had gone there, and who had worn on his legs and arms cascabels that jingled. The black man had been killed, and had been cut into pieces, which were distributed among many headmen so that they could be convinced he was not a god, not a child of the sun, but a mortal.

When he reached the Coana tribes, Alarcon found them disturbed by news, which recently had reached them, that a large army of men who wore beards had invaded Cibola and had conquered the province.

In this way Alarcon learned that Estevanico had perished, and that Coronado had reached the Seven Cities.

In vain Alarcon attempted to send messengers to Cibola to inform Coronado of his whereabouts. Both his own men and Indians refused to undertake the mission. It was their reasoning that the Cibolans would not welcome the news that more Spaniards were approaching.

Defeated in his effort to reach Coronado, Alarcon reluctantly returned downstream to his ships.

Meanwhile, Coronado had been attempting to find Alarcon and obtain the supplies so badly needed. He had sent Diaz to look for him.

In September, 1540, with twenty-five soldiers and a similar number of Opatas, Diaz had left San Geronimo de los Corazones, in Sonora, and headed westward . . . across the unexplored deserts of northern Mexico and southern Arizona, a trail so difficult and terrible that it would come to be known as the Devil's Highway.

Reaching the Gila's mouth, Diaz turned south, intending to descend the left bank of the Colorado to the sea, the Gulf of California. En route he received word from Cocopa Indians which sent his hopes soaring. Spaniards, they told him, in small boats had ascended the river to a place "fifteen leagues from the head of the bay."

Tense with suspense, Diaz and his men hurried on southward. On the third day of travel down the river, the sharp eyes of their guides picked out a tree which appeared to have been blazed. Upon reaching it, Diaz read the words, carved in the tree wood:

Alarcon came this far. There are
letters at the foot of this tree.

All hopes were destroyed by the content of the letters. They said that Alarcon had gone back.

Reporting to Viceroy Mendoza what he had learned of Estevanico's death from a Cocopa Indian, Alarcon said: "He told me that the chief of that country [Cibola] had a dog similar to the one I had with me [a greyhound]. Having expressed a desire to eat, this man seeing the plates brought in, said that the chief of Cibola had similar ones, but that they were green, and that the chief was the only one who owned such plates. He had four of them, which had been given to him, together with the dog, by a man who was black... He [the Cocopa] did not know when this man had come [to Cibola], but he had been told that the chief of Cibola had caused him to be killed.

"Your Lordship will remember that the negro who accompanied Fray Marcos had rattles (bells), and feathers on his arms and legs; that he had plates of different colors, and that he came to this country a little more than a year ago."

Alarcon had asked the Cocopa why Estevanico had been killed, and the Cocopa had replied:

"The chief of Cibola having asked him whether he had other brethren, the negro replied that he had an infinite number, that they carried many weapons, and were not very far off. Upon this statement a great many chiefs gathered in council, and agreed on killing the negro, so that he might not impart any information to his brethren in regard to the country of Cibola. Such was the cause of his death. His body was cut into a great many pieces, which were distributed among all the chiefs in order that they might know that he was surely dead."

XVII

UNTIL THE ARRIVAL of Coronado in Hawikuh, the story
which Fray Marcos had brought back to Mexico City
had been the only account of Estevanico's death known
to the Viceroy. Coronado soon obtained information
which left no doubt that the friar's report of the tragedy
was not only inaccurate but in some respects was completely false.

In his August, 1540, letter to Mendoza, Coronado
wrote: "The death of the negro is perfectly certain, because many of the things which he wore have been
found, and the Indians say that they killed him here
because the Indians at Chichilticale said he was a bad
man, and not like the Christians, because the Christians
never kill women, and he killed them, and because he as-
saulted their women, whom the Indians love better than
themselves.

"Therefore they determined to kill him, *but they did not do it in the way that was reported* [by Fray Marcos], *because they did not kill any of the others who came with him, nor did they kill the lad from the province of Petatlan, who was with him, but they took him and kept him in safe custody . . .*"

The lad from Petatlan was Bartolome, Estevanico's faithful personal servant. Coronado secured his release from the Zunis, and assigned him to his staff of interpreters.

Fray Marcos's fabrication that some three hundred persons with Estevanico had been slain by the Zunis was valuable to him for two reasons:

First, by going on in the face of such peril until he could see Hawikuh from a distant rise, his courage was demonstrated, his dedication to duty was evidenced.

Second, with Estevanico and all the other men and women slaughtered, it would have been the height of idiocy for him to have attempted to enter the pueblo.

Castaneda, who was in Cibola with the army of Coronado, threw a revealing light on the slaying of Estevanico with these words:

"As I said, Estevan reached Cibola loaded with the large quantity of turquoises they had given him and some beautiful women whom the Indians who followed him and carried his things were taking with them and had given him. These had followed him from all the settlements he had passed, believing that under his protection they could traverse the whole world without any danger.

"But as the people in this country [Cibola] were more intelligent than those who followed Estevan, they lodged him in a little hut they had outside their village, and the older men and the governors heard his story and took steps to find out the reason he had come to that country.

"For three days they made inquiries about him and held a council."

For *three* days they deliberated. Fray Marcos had said that when Estevanico reached Hawikuh he was only *three* days behind him. If that were true, why hadn't he arrived within sight of the pueblo either on the day of Estevanico's death or the day immediately following it?

Of course, it was not true. At the time Estevanico perished, Fray Marcos was more than a hundred miles from Hawikuh, perhaps as much as a hundred and fifty miles from it.

And Castaneda continued: "The account which the negro gave them of two white men who were following him, sent by a great lord, who knew about the things in the sky, and how these were coming to instruct them in divine matters, made them think that he must be a spy or a guide from some nations who wished to come and conquer them, because it seemed to them unreasonable to say that the people were white in the country from which he came and that he was sent by them, he being black.*

"Besides these other reasons, they thought it was hard of him to ask them for turquoises and women, and so they decided to kill him.

*Castaneda obviously had forgotten that only one white man was following Estevanico, that Fray Onorato had been left behind because of illness. But Estevanico may well have said there were two white men. He may have said, and probably did, that many white men were coming, for he was fully apprised of the preparations being made by Coronado.

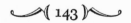

"This they did, *but they did not kill any of those who went with him*, although they kept some young fellows and let the others, about sixty persons [from the Valle de Sonora] return freely to their own country.

"As these, who were badly scared, were returning in flight, they happened to come upon the friars in the desert *sixty leagues from Cibola*, and told them the sad news."

The Spanish judicial league equaled 2.634 English miles. Thus, according to Castaneda, Fray Marcos was more than one hundred and fifty miles from Hawikuh when he met Indians bearing the news that Estevanico was dead.

Castaneda tells what happened when Fray Marcos met these fleeing people: "The friars were now seized with such fear that they could not even trust these folk who had been with the negro, [and] they opened their bags they were carrying and gave away everything they had, except the holy vestments for saying mass.

"*From there* [more than a hundred and fifty miles from Hawikuh] *the friars turned back by forced marches*, with their gowns up to their waists . . . without seeing anything more of the country . . ."

Fray Marcos, honored in history as the discoverer of Arizona, New Mexico and the Seven Cities of Cibola, discovered nothing.

He did not get farther north in Arizona than the Gila River. He did not set a sandaled foot in territory that would become the State of New Mexico. He never saw Hawikuh.

The discoverer of Arizona, New Mexico and Cibola was Estevanico the Black.

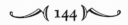

He died at Hawikuh on a May morning in 1539, when the sun was only a lance high.

The Zuni Indians who killed him kept his turquoises, his corals, his feathers and his bells, his greyhounds and his green dinner plates.

They threw away the sacred gourd rattle.

* * * * *

The stones of Hawikuh still lie scattered over the gentle rise on which it stood when Estevanico the Black found it.

Perhaps some historical society might be induced to gather a few of these stones and fashion a monument in his memory. A small crude one would do.

BIBLIOGRAPHY

Arteaga, y S., Armando, FRAY MARCOS DE NIZA Y EL DESCUBRI-
MIENTO DE NUEVO MEXICO, Hispanic American Historical Review, Vol. XII, November, 1932.

Baldwin, Percy M., FRAY MARCOS DE NIZA AND HIS DISCOVERY
OF THE SEVEN CITIES OF CIBOLA, New Mexico Historical Review, Vol. I, April, 1926.

Bancroft, Hubert Howe, HISTORY OF THE NORTH MEXICAN STATES
AND TEXAS, 2 vols., San Francisco, 1884.

————, ARIZONA AND NEW MEXICO, 1530-1888, San Francisco,
1888.

Bandelier, Adolph F., ALVAR NUNEZ CABEZA DE VACA, THE FIRST
OVERLAND TRAVELER OF EUROPEAN DESCENT, AND HIS JOUR-
NEY FROM FLORIDA TO THE PACIFIC COAST, 1528-1536, Maga-
zine of Western History, Vol. IV, July, 1886.

————, CONTRIBUTIONS TO THE HISTORY OF THE SOUTHWESTERN
PORTION OF THE UNITED STATES, Paper of the Archeological Institute of America, American Series, Vol. V, Cambridge, 1890.

Bandelier, Adolph F. (*Continued*)

————, The Discovery of New Mexico by Fray Marcos of Niza, Magazine of Western History, Vol. IV, September, 1886. Reprinted in the New Mexico Historical Review, Vol. IV, January, 1929.

————, The Gilded Man, New York, 1893.

Bandelier, Fanny, The Journey of Alvar Nunez Cabeza de Vaca and His Companions from Florida to the Pacific, 1528-1536. Translation of the 1542 edition of Cabeza de Vaca's Relacion. New York, 1905.

Bartlett, Katherine, and Harold S. Colton, A Note on the Marcos de Niza Inscription Near Phoenix, Arizona, *Plateau*, Vol. XII, April, 1940.

Baskett, James Newton, A Study of the Route of Cabeza de Vaca, Texas Historical Association Quarterly, Vol. X, January-April, 1907.

Bishop, Morris, The Odyssy of Cabeza de Vaca, New York, 1933.

Bloom, Lansing B., Was Fray Marcos a Liar? New Mexico Historical Review, Vol. XVI, April, 1941.

————, Who Discovered New Mexico?, New Mexico Historical Review, Vol. XV, April, 1940.

Bolton, Herbert Eugene, The Spanish Borderlands, Chronicles of America, Vol. XXIII, New Haven, 1921.

————, Coronado, Knight of Pueblo and Plains, Albuquerque and New York, 1949. Reprinted, 1964.

————, Spanish Explorations in the Southwest, New York, 1916.

Brackenridge, H. M., Early Discoveries by the Spaniards in New Mexico, Containing an Account of the Castles of Cibola, Pittsburgh, 1857.

Cabeza de Vaca, Alvar Nunez, La Relacion Que Dio Alvar Nunez Cabeca de Vaca de lo Acaescido en las Indias en la Armada Donde Yua Por Gouernador Pamphilo de Narvaez, Zamora, Spain, 1540. (See Bandelier, Hodge, Smith, Winship.)

Cabeza de Vaca, Alvar Nunez *(Continued)*

————, Cabeza de Vaca, Alvar Nunez, Alonzo del Castillo Maldonado and Andres Dorantes de Carranca, Joint Report, summarized by Oviedo y Valdez, q.v.

Castaneda, Pedro de, Relacion de la Journada de Cibola con Puesta por e Pedro de Castaneda de Nacera Donde se Trata de Todos Aqueleos Porlados y Ritos Costumbres, la Cical Fue el Ano de 1540, Translated by Winship, q.v., Fourteenth Annual Report of the Bureau of American Ethnology, Washington, 1896.

Cushing, Frank Hamilton, Zuni Folk Tales, New York, 1901. (See Hodge, Handbook, etc.)

Davenport, Harbert, The Expedition of Panfilo de Narvaez, Southwestern Historical Quarterly, Vol. XXVIII, October, 1924.

————, and Joseph K. Wells, The First Europeans in Texas, Southwestern Historical Quarterly, Vol. XXII, October, 1918.

Espejo, Antonio, see Bolton, Spanish Explorations in the Southwest.

Farnum, Mabel, The Seven Golden Cities, Milwaukee, 1943.

Hallenbeck, Cleve, Alvar Nunez Cabeza de Vaca: The Journey and Route of the First European to Cross the Continent of North America, 1534-1536, Glendale, 1939.

Hammond, George P., Coronado's Seven Cities, Albuquerque, 1940.

———— and Agapito Rey, The Narratives of the Coronado Expedition, 1540-1542, Aubuquerque, 1940.

———— and Edgar F. Goad, The Adventure of Don Francisco Vasquez de Coronado, Albuquerque, 1938.

Hodge, Frederick W., The First Discovered City of Cibola, *American Anthropologist*, Vol. XIII, April, 1895.

————, Handbook of American Indians North of Mexico, 2 Vols., Bulletin No. 30, American Bureau of Ethnology, Washington, 1907.

Hodge, Frederick W. *(Continued)*

————, HISTORY OF HAWIKUH, NEW MEXICO, ONE OF THE SO-CALLED CITIES OF CIBOLA, Los Angeles, 1937.

———— and Theodore H. Lewis, eds., SPANISH EXPLORERS IN THE SOUTHERN UNITED STATES, New York, 1907. Reprinted 1959. Contains Cabeza de Vaca's RELACION and Castaneda's CORONADO, in English translation, with footnotes.

Lummis, Charles F., THE SPANISH PIONEERS, Chicago, 1893.

Marcos de Niza, Fray, RELACION DEL DESCUBRIMIENTO DE LAS SIETE CIUDADES. See Baldwin, Bandelier, Hammond.

Morgan, Lewis Henry, THE SEVEN CITIES OF CIBOLA, North American Review, Vol. CVIII, April, 1869.

Oviedo y Valdez, Gonzalo de Fernandez de, LA HISTORIA GEN-ERAL DE LAS INDIES, Seville, 1535.

Sauer, Carl O., THE CREDIBILITY OF THE FRAY MARCOS ACCOUNT, New Mexico Historical Review, Vol. XVI, April, 1941.

————, THE DISCOVERY OF NEW MEXICO RECONSIDERED, New Mexico Historical Review, Vol. XII, July, 1937.

————, THE ROAD TO CIBOLA, *Ibero-Americana* No. 3, Berkeley, 1930.

Smith, T. Buckingham, RELACION OF ALVAR NUNEZ CABEZA DE VACA, Translated from the 1555 edition, which was printed at Valladolid, Washington, 1851.

Terrell, John Upton, JOURNEY INTO DARKNESS, New York, 1962.

————, CABEZA DE VACA'S TOWN OF THE HEARTS, Palm Desert, Calif., 1965.

Twitchell, Ralph Emerson, LEADING FACTS OF NEW MEXICAN HISTORY, 5 Vols., Cedar Rapids, Iowa, 1911.

Undreimer, George J., FRAY MARCOS DE NIZA, HIS JOURNEY TO CIBOLA, *The Americas,* Vol. III, April, 1947.

Wagner, Henry R., FR. MARCOS DE NIZA, New Mexico Historical Review, Vol. IX, April, 1934.

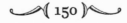

Wagner, Henry R. *(Continued)*

————, A FRAY MARCOS DE NIZA NOTE, New Mexico Historical Review, Vol. IX, July, 1934.

Winship, George Parker, THE CORONADO EXPEDITION, 1540-1542, Fourteenth Annual Report of the Bureau of American Ethnology, Washington, 1896.

————, THE JOURNEY OF CORONADO, New York, 1904.

————, WHY CORONADO WENT TO NEW MEXICO IN 1540, Annual Report of the American Historical Association, 1894, Washington, 1895.

INDEX

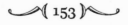

BOOKS OF THE WEST . . . FROM THE WEST

DATE DUE	BORROWER'S NAME

DATE DUE	BORROWER'S NAME